THE ESSENTIAL
LIGHTING
MANUAL FOR
DIGITAL AND FILM
PHOTOGRAPHERS

A RotoVision Book

Published and distributed by RotoVision SA
Route Suisse 9
CH-1295 Mies
Switzerland

RotoVision SA
Sales, Editorial & Production Office
Sheridan House
112/116A Western Road
Brighton & Hove
BN3 1DD
UK

Tel: +44 (0)1273 72 72 68
Fax: +44 (0)1273 72 72 69
Email: sales@rotovision.com
Web: www.rotovision.com

10 9 8 7 6 5 4 3 2 1

ISBN: 2-88046-763-2

Art Director Luke Herriott
Book designed by Richard Wolfströme
Cover designed by Mark Roberts

Reprographics in Singapore by
ProVision Pte. Ltd
Tel: +65 6334 7720
Fax: +65 6334 7721

Printing and Binding in China by
Midas Printing International

THE ESSENTIAL
LIGHTING
MANUAL FOR
DIGITAL AND FILM
PHOTOGRAPHERS

Chris Weston

RotoVision

CONTENTS

INTRODUCTION

0.1

WHAT YOU SEE IS NOT NECESSARILY WHAT YOU GET

Before you read this book, put it down and try this little exercise.

Look at a scene in front of you and close one eye. It doesn't matter which one. Now, with your open eye, squint and take some time to examine what you're seeing. Notice the lack of information that you have available to you. Can you see how much more difficult it is to distinguish distance from, and separation between, objects? How contrast between light and dark has increased, with detail-less blacks and whites? And how objects that before appeared three-dimensional now appear flat?

Okay, you can open both eyes now. What's the point of this exercise? Well, what you just saw is pretty much exactly what your camera would have seen if pointed at the same scene. You see, the key to great photography is the ability to visualize the image you are trying to create

and to distinguish between how we see light as bi-optic, thinking beings, and how cameras see light as one-eyed, inanimate tools.

In a nutshell, that is what this book is all about—seeing light and learning how to use it effectively.

Light is the photographer's primary tool. Without it there would be no photographs. Yet it is amazing to me how many would-be photographers take light for granted, or imagine that there is only one way to light a subject. Here's an example. I was taking photographs of Alnwick Castle in Northumberland, England, and had been for the best part of a week. One morning a young man arrived, set up his tripod and, within a few minutes, had fired some shots and packed away his gear. Just before he set off, he said, "Well, that's the castle done." I simply nodded, dumbfounded, and turned back to my own camera.

My point is this: I took several photographs of Alnwick Castle that week, and not one is the same. In each, the light is different, lending every picture a unique mood and a different story. Each one says, "This is what Alnwick Castle looked like on this day, at this time, and under these conditions." This is the wonder of photography.

How we illustrate these moments is through our interpretation and manipulation of light. Light gives photographs character. It transforms them from two-dimensional images on paper to three-dimensional embodiments—not only of the scene before you—but your personal interpretation of it, molded by your experiences, emotions, and desires. Without an ability to control light you can't stamp your photographs with your own imprint, and they will rarely live up to your expectations.

So, learning how to use light to its maximum potential is a fundamental requirement if you are to get beyond the confines of technical mediocrity, and set yourself apart from the photographic also-rans. The fact that you have gotten this far is enough to tell me that you want your pictures to say something different. In essence, you want your photographs to have that something special that might be called the "wow" factor.

0.1 *African sunset, Kruger National Park, South Africa.*

0.2—0.4 *These images of Alnwick Castle were all taken on the same day. Notice how the changing light, as well as perspective, gives each a completely different visual presence from the other.*

0.2

0.3

0.4

Let me give you a feel for what to expect from the rest of this book. On a recent photographic workshop, I was explaining the intricacies of calculating exposure. It took just ten minutes. At the end of the workshop, one of the delegates came up to me and said, "Thanks for a great day and thank you for the most informative and simple-to-apply explanation of exposure I've ever heard. If only people would write books that way."

Well, the comment pleased me so much I decided to do just that. And, while not solely about exposure, this book is written, I hope, to counter and clarify the overly technical approaches on lighting for photography that do nothing to demystify the subject. I am not predisposed to complicated, scientific tomes. I want a manual to give me information I can follow easily and readily apply in the field or studio.

In these pages, you will find straightforward explanations of the nature of light and lighting, uncomplicated guidance on lighting techniques throughout the day, the seasons of the year, and other conditions, well-informed examples of how to handle complex lighting situations, and clear supporting diagrams of studio set-ups. But, throughout, by keeping things simple, and as jargon-free as possible (without losing the complexity), I don't stray too far away from the main point, the reason we are photographers: because we enjoy it!

As your ability to understand and manipulate photography's basic ingredient—light—develops, always remind yourself of the sheer joy that is the art of photography, and that will see you through. I have enjoyed writing this book, and hope that my own love of photography, and of light, shines through, and helps you to remember why you want to know more.

0.5 *Light gives your pictures character and can turn what would be an ordinary portrait shot into a photograph full of emotion.*

0.5

UNDERSTANDING LIGHT

When you woke up this morning and went about your daily routine you saw things. In fact, you saw any number of things until you shut your eyes to go to sleep. And everything you saw was entirely dependent on one thing: light.

Light is all your eyes ever see. Whether you are admiring the landscape or works of art, watching children play, or marveling at the beauty of comets and shooting stars, what you are actually seeing is reflected light.

Of course, exactly the same can be said of the camera. In its simplest form, when you open the eye—the lens aperture—of the camera, an image is formed and recorded on light-sensitive material. The camera has no concept of the subject's form or being, it simply records the different waves of light that pass through the lens.

So, what we see and what the camera records is light, and understanding how light works is the basis for mastering the photographic art.

HOW LIGHT WORKS

This section is a tiny bit technical, but bear with me because it is essential to understanding the photographic process and enabling you to capture compelling images.

For simplicity, I refer to light in terms of waves, since this gives the best explanation for the many ways in which we observe light. In relation to photography, there are two important things to consider. Firstly, waves come in many different sizes and we can see only a very small fraction of wavelengths—known as "visible light" (see 1.1). Secondly, light waves also come in many frequencies, and it is these frequencies that, in visible light, give us color.

The color of light

Six principal colors, or lights of different frequencies, are visible to the naked eye: red, orange, yellow, green, blue, and violet. Mixing some of these colors produces many more colors—or frequencies— and combining all the colors in the visible spectrum will produce white, colorless light.

Colors by addition

One way of making colors is by adding two or more together. For example, let's take red, green, and blue. Mixing equal parts of red and blue will give you magenta. The same combination of blue and green will produce cyan, and green and red will produce yellow. An equal mix of all three will take us back to white (see 1.2). By adding various combinations of red, green, and blue light, all the colors of the visible spectrum can be produced, and this is how computer monitors (RGB monitors) produce colors.

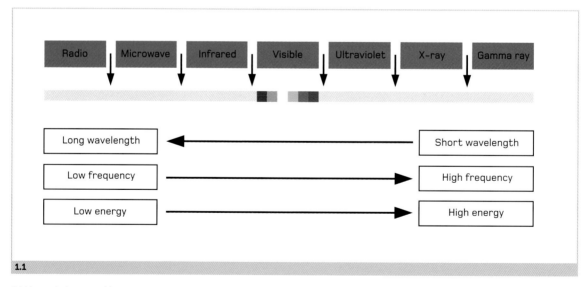

1.1

1.1 *Human beings are able to see only "visible" light waves. Film and digital photo sensors, on the other hand, can be sensitive to other elements of the electro-magnetic spectrum, such as ultraviolet light.*

1.2

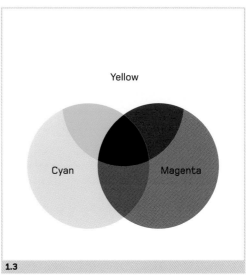

1.3

Colors by subtraction

Color is also made another way, by absorbing some of the light frequencies, removing them from the combination. This is how paint and color dye is produced, and it can be witnessed in nature. For example, the leaves of green plants contain a pigment called chlorophyll which *absorbs* blue and red from the light spectrum while *reflecting* green— hence the apparent color of green leaves.

Now, think back to the days of the color darkroom, or take a look at the inks in your color printer. A color enlarger has three color dials: yellow, magenta, and cyan (which, by the way, match the principal inks used in basic color printing). Mixing an equal portion of yellow and cyan will produce green; cyan and magenta will produce blue, and magenta and yellow will produce red. Where all three are mixed equally, all light frequencies are absorbed and you get black (see 1.3).

This method of color by subtraction is also how color correction filters work in combination with photographic film and photo sensors.

Color temperature

Color is often referred to in terms of its temperature. For example, blue light is described as being cool (we associate blue with ice, for instance), while red light is described as being warm (and is often associated with fire). In reality, the human eye automatically compensates for variances in color temperature and we often find one temperature of light indistinguishable from another. However, light-sensitive materials such as photographic film, record these temperatures with far less latitude, thus it is important that you are able to identify the temperature of different types of light source and, with sunlight, at different times of the day.

Light temperature can be measured using a scale known as the Kelvin scale (K). Midday summer sunlight on a clear day, for example, is around 5,500K. On the same summer day, however, the temperature of light around sunset is only about 2,000K— far warmer than the bluer midday light. The table (see page 15) provides an outline of color temperatures under different lighting conditions.

1.2 *It is possible to produce millions of colors by adding combinations of red, green, and blue. This is how color computer monitors work.*

1.3 *Alternatively, color can be made by subtraction, which is how photographic enlargers and computer printers work.*

1.4

1.5

Reflected light

I have explained that what the camera records through the lens, is reflected light. Well, here's another science bit. Light is a form of energy made up of "photons", which are produced by energizing "electrons" orbiting the nucleus of an atom. When light falls on an object, its reaction depends on a number of things, including the energy of the light wave, the frequency at which electrons vibrate in the subject material, and the strength with which the atoms in the subject material hold on to their electrons. Based on these factors, when light falls on an object it will respond in one of the following ways: through transparency, absorption, reflectance, scattering, refraction, and multiple-surface reflectance.

Transparency

When the energy of the light is far greater or far lower than the frequency needed to make the subject material vibrate, then the light will pass straight through, and the object is considered transparent (see 1.6), which is what happens with glass objects.

Absorption

When the frequency of the incoming light is similar to that of the vibration frequency of the subject material, then light is absorbed. The absorption of light makes an object dark or opaque to the frequency of the light wave. This is what happens with wood, which is opaque to visible light, and glass, which is opaque to ultraviolet light (although transparent to visible light) (see 1.7).

Light source	Color temperature
Shaded subject in sunlight	8,000K
Overcast sky	7,000K
Lightly overcast sky	6,000K
Summer sunlight	5,500K
Early morning/late afternoon sun	3,500K
Photographic flash	3,400K
Tungsten halogen lamp	3,200K
Household light bulb	2,800K
Sunset	2,000K

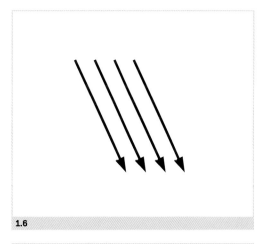

1.6

1.7

1.4 & 1.5 *The color of light affects our emotional response to a picture. Compare these two images. How much warmer does the picture above feel compared to the picture below?*

1.6 *Transparency.*

1.7 *Absorption.*

Reflectance

Where a subject material consists of atoms that hold on to their electrons loosely, light waves end up being reflected by the surface. This is the case with most metals, which appear shiny to the eye. In this instance, the incoming light waves are reflected at the same angle and frequency. In physics, this is referred to as the "Law of Reflectance". A perfect example of this is a mirror. If you look in a mirror, you will see that the colors of your clothes are exactly the same in the reflection as they are in real life.

Scattering

Reflectance is the result of light waves bouncing off a smooth surface. When the surface is rough, however, then you get scattering, with the light waves reflecting in an indiscriminate pattern. The earth's atmosphere is a good example of a rough surface, being made up of molecules of different sizes, such as oxygen, water vapor, and pollutants. The different molecules scatter the light waves we see as blue (high energy), which is why the sky appears blue.

1.8 *Reflectance.*

1.9 *Scattering.*

1.10 *Light scattering from the rough surface of the earth's atmosphere causes the sky to appear blue.*

1.8

1.9

1.10

1.11

1.12

1.11 & 1.12 *Refraction.
Bending light is responsible
for the order of colors in
a rainbow.*

1.13 *Refraction.*

Refraction

When the natural vibration frequency
of the subject material matches that
of the light wave, then refraction
occurs. Without getting into the
technicalities, what this means is
that the light bends inside the
object. Refraction can be very clearly
seen in objects such as diamonds
and crystals. Refraction is also
responsible for the order of colors
in a rainbow. This is because light
of different frequencies bends at
slightly different angles (see 1.13).

1.13

Multiple-surface reflectance

Have you ever noticed the rainbow colors in soap bubbles, or the rainbow patterns on oil spills on a wet road? This is caused by light waves passing through an object with two reflective surfaces. Take the oil spill as an example. The oil reflects parts of the light waves, while others penetrate the oil and are reflected by the road surface. This forces them out of sync and they interfere with each other, leading to the formation of a new color, or frequency.

1.14

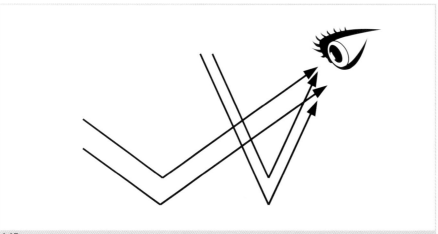

1.15

1.14 *On a cloudy day, the sun acts as a diffused light source. However, when entering through a small window, such as the one seen in this church, the window turns the soft diffused light into a point source.*

1.15 *Multiple-surface reflectance.*

1.16

INTENSITY OF LIGHT

The intensity of light depends on two criteria: the distance between the light source and the subject, and the size of the light source.

The closer the light source is to the subject, the greater the intensity of light and illumination. Moving the light source closer or farther away from the subject alters the level of light falling on the subject. For example, if you halve the distance between your subject and a point light source, such as a small flash unit, you will increase by four times the amount of light reaching the subject (this is referred to as the "inverse square law"). Halving the distance between the light source and the subject quadruples the illumination, and doubling it reduces illumination to one quarter. In photographic practice, this allows you greater control over exposure settings since more light gives you greater choice of lens aperture/shutter speed combinations.

A practical result of the inverse square law is exposing multiple subjects at varying distances from a point light source. For example, if one subject is twice as far away from the light source as a second subject, then it will receive only a quarter of the illumination, and will require an exposure four times as long. Depending on your photographic material, this may not be possible. One solution is to move the light source *much* farther away, so that the ratio of nearest-to-farthest distance is reduced.

By way of example, when photographing outdoors in direct sunlight the inverse square law no longer applies, because the distance between the sun and different points of the earth—the summit and base of a mountain, for example—is so great that, to all intents and purposes, all surfaces will receive the same intensity of light, and variations will only be caused by atmospheric conditions.

TIP

When using natural light indoors with the sun entering through a doorway or window, the opening will act as a compact point light source and light intensity will alter with distance.

1.16 *Light from a point source illuminates your subject at four times the brightness with every halving of the distance between the light and the subject. Inversely, every doubling of the light-to-subject distance will reduce illumination by one quarter. This is known as the "inverse square law".*

1.17

Size of light source

Another solution is to alter the size of the light source. The size of your light source is governed by two things: the physical size, and its distance from the subject being photographed. Distance is important. Take the sun, for example. The sun is a massive light source but, being so far away from the earth, it acts like a small point light source. However, add some cloud cover and the effect is much like adding a soft box to a flash unit, turning the point source into a larger source of light.

The size of the light source will determine the effect created. Small light sources are referred to as "hard" because they produce hard-edged shadows and high contrast. Large light sources are considered "soft" because shadows are poorly defined and levels of contrast are reduced. Of course, as with most things in photography, "hard" and "soft" lighting can be measured in degrees, with multiple variations in between the extremes.

Now, back to the inverse square law: because light travels in straight lines, the fall-off of light is most pronounced when photographing using a point light source, such as a flash unit or direct sunlight. By diffusing a point light source—as described above— you create a more even spread of light across a wider area.

1.17—1.19 *Light from a point source tends to create a higher level of contrast than that from a diffused light source. Compare these three images. The first image, (1.17), was taken with a diffused light source. The second, (1.18), was taken with a point light source. The last, (1.19), was taken with a heavily directed point source. Notice how the shadows appear softer in the first image, becoming gradually harder as the light source becomes more direct.*

1.18

1.19

1.20

DIFFUSION

Diffusing light has two main purposes. I have discussed the first purpose by explaining how a diffused light source provides more even illumination over a wider surface area. The second reason you may want to diffuse light is to soften shadow areas in a picture. For example, when light comes from a single point and reaches a subject, the shut-off of illumination is sudden and pronounced. However, when light is diffused, the direct light scatters into many more light points emanating in all directions from the area of diffusion. Some of this extra light will fall around the subject, rather than directly onto it, and areas previously in full shadow will receive at least some illumination.

In outdoor photography, this is where atmospheric conditions come into play. A prime example of a diffused light source is sunlight on a cloudy day. The sun acts as a point light source but as soon as that light hits the clouds it scatters in very many new straight lines of light. The same is achieved with artificial light by bouncing the flash light off a large wall or umbrella, or by using a sheet of opaque material such as a soft box directly in front of the light source.

TIP

How light affects the type of shadows created is sometimes referred to as the "quality" of light. Hard light, i.e. that coming from a direct, compact light source, causes sharp-edged, dark shadows. Soft light, such as sunlight on an overcast day, produces soft, graduated shadows.

1.20 & 1.21 *The strength of the shadow is determined by the size of the light source. A point (small) light source will produce dark, well-defined shadows, such as that seen in 1.20, while a diffused (large) light source will give light shadows with softer edges, as shown in 1.21.*

1.22 *Even on an overcast day, a small window can turn a large point source into a direct point source.*

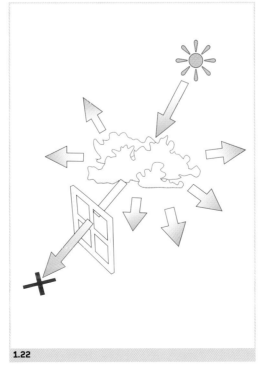

1.22

NOTE

A diffused light source can be turned back into a point light source by blocking much of the light and allowing just a small amount to pass through onto the subject. For instance, in an earlier example I explained how, when photographing indoors under natural light, a window or doorway would act as a point light source. This would be true in overcast conditions where the solid walls surrounding the opening would block a large amount of the light present from reaching the subject.

CONTRAST

Another condition affected by the type of lighting used is contrast. Contrast refers to the difference in brightness between the shadow areas and highlight areas of your subject. When we look at a scene or subject, our eyes automatically compensate for different levels of brightness and we can see detail with a high degree of latitude. Photosensitive material, however, is far less clever and has only a narrow latitude. For example, positive (transparency) film has latitude of about five stops, negative film about seven stops, and digital photo sensors eight stops.

So, if you were photographing a scene using positive film, where the shadow areas were six stops darker than the highlight areas, it would be impossible, without additional fill-in lighting, to record detail in both highlight and shadow.

Contrast is greatest when using direct lighting from the side or directly above the subject. You can see, then, that photographing a landscape on a bright, sunny day around noon will give an image with a lot of contrast. This is one of the reasons that landscape photographers prefer not to shoot at midday.

NOTE

Contrast can be used to great creative effect. One of photography's greatest practitioners, Ansel Adams, was a master at employing contrast to create dramatic, powerful landscape images.

1.23 & 1.24

1.23 & 1.24 Using additional fill-in lighting, or a reflector, is a very effective way to lighten dark shadow areas, revealing detail and enhancing your picture.

1.25 & 1.26 Compare these images. The first, taken of a puffin on a cloudless day, has created a level of contrast too broad for the film to cope with, and the white feathers have washed out. The shot of the penguins, however, was taken on an overcast day. The diffused lighting has reduced the level of contrast to within the film's latitude, which means that the detail remains in both black and white feathers.

1.26

1.25

1.27

1.27 The direction of your light source plays an important part in the rendering of texture and detail in your final image.

DIRECTION OF LIGHT

The direction of the light source relative to your subject will also play a key part in how that subject is rendered in the final image. A light's direction will dictate, for instance, how surface detail appears: flat or textured, and how and where shadows fall, which will determine the sense of depth in your picture. You can also exploit the direction of light for artistic effect, creating silhouettes or beautiful golden "halos" that punctuate subject features and provide a frame of emphasis.

Typically, the direction of the light source will be either from the front, back, side, or above, and I explain how each affects the composition of your image, opposite. There are occasions when you may use lighting from below, usually in commercial fields where shadow-free images are required.

1.28 Front lighting.

1.29 Side lighting.

1.30 Backlighting.

1.28

1.29

1.30

1.31

1.31 *The use of frontal lighting for this portrait gives it a much flatter appearance.*

1.32

1.32 *The addition of side lighting on this portrait brings form to the image, accentuating the curves of the model's body.*

1.33

1.33 *The addition of a backlight has added highlights that create contrast and produce a more interesting portrait.*

Frontal lighting

You may have been given the age-old advice to always shoot with the sun behind you. This was based on the limitations of "point and shoot" cameras and was universally ignored by most experienced photographers because, while it ensured the greatest level of illumination (or intensity), thereby giving an accurate rendition of surface features, it also created flat, dull pictures. Frontal lighting generally eradicates shadow from a photograph, and shadows help to give an image depth. The lack of contrast from frontal lighting also flattens surface detail and is of no use when you are trying to emphasize texture in a photograph. If, however, you are simply trying to record features in a scene, then front lighting will provide you with adequate lighting conditions.

Overhead- and side-lighting

A good method for emphasizing texture or form is to use overhead- or side-lighting. Lighting coming from above or to the side of the subject creates shadow areas that punctuate, for example, the undulations in the bark of a tree, or distinguish between the sides of a three-dimensional object, such as a building.

Backlighting

Backlighting can be used to exploit the differences in reflectivity. For example, water, when backlit, appears wet and liquid, as you would expect. However, when lit by overhead- or side-lighting, it appears more solid. Creatively, backlighting can be used to produce the "golden halo" effect often seen in portraits. One thing to be aware of when using backlighting is the possibility of lens flare caused by light falling directly onto the lens. A lens hood will help to reduce these effects.

NOTE

THE KEY POINTS

The temperature of light affects the color balance in your photographs and can be controlled to some degree by your choice of film or, with digital cameras, the White Balance setting.

The surface of the subject material determines how the light falling on it is reflected. Recognizing the reflective properties of your subject will help you visualize how it will appear in the final image.

Using artificial light, the bigger and closer the light source it is to the subject, the greater the intensity of light and the flexibility you have to set lens aperture and shutter speed. However, under natural light conditions, the intensity of light is only affected by atmospheric conditions.

Direct light (natural or artificial) creates hard-edged shadows and increases the level of contrast in a scene. Diffused light, on the other hand, lowers levels of contrast and gives soft-edged shadows.

Film and digital photo sensors can only record detail across narrow latitude between featureless black and white. Therefore, in high-contrast scenes, you must either compensate for the shadows using fill-flash or reflectors, compensate for the highlights using neutral density filters, or choose between recording detail in the shadow areas or in the highlight areas.

Frontal lighting is the best option when an accurate rendition of surface features is required. To emphasize texture and form, overhead or side-lighting is a better option.

NOTE

COMMON ERRORS TO AVOID

Avoid conflicting shadows. Only one set of shadows should be visible and they should point in the same direction. Where it is impossible to avoid conflicting shadows, use the techniques described in this section to soften the edges of shadows.

When photographing portraits, try to light the background separately from the subject. This will avoid shadows on the backdrop that will detract from your composition.

Where shadows occur, include them in your composition. A large black area apparently disengaged from the subject will overpower the scene and detract from the overall picture design.

When using backlighting, use a lens hood to help minimize the effects of lens flare.

1.34

1.34 *When photographing portraits, light the background separately to avoid casting shadow on your subject that will detract from the composition.*

METERING AND EXPOSURE

Having got to grips with the physics of light, this chapter looks at the relationship between light and the camera. We know that when reflected light falls on light-sensitive material an image will form on it.

Unfortunately, photography is a little more complicated than that—the next step is determining exactly how much light you need to allow to fall on the film or photo sensor, and for how long.

2.1

2.2

HOW LIGHT IS MEASURED

Light can be measured in one of two ways: by assessing the brightness of the scene (reflected light), or the amount of light falling on the scene (incident light). The light meter then calculates an exposure value, which in turn can be translated (either by the meter or by you) into a combination of lens aperture and shutter speed. The light reading will always be given in relation to the film speed or ISO equivalency you've set.

The basics are simple enough, but in practice there are some influencing factors that need to be taken into account if you are to calculate an accurate reading. The best place to start is by gaining an understanding of the different types of light meter and how each works.

There are two types of natural light meter: an incident light meter and a reflected light meter. A third type of light meter, a flash meter, used to calculate electronic flash exposure values, is often used in studio photography (see page 45).

2.3

2.1 & 2.2 *Incident light meters measure the amount of light falling onto a subject. For best results, it should be placed near to the subject and pointed toward the camera.*

2.3 *Hand-held reflected light meters assess the amount of light reflected directly from the subject.*

2.4 *Built into the camera, a TTL meter measures the amount of light entering the lens. Because it takes into account any attachments, such as filters, extenders and extension tubes, it is one of the most accurate forms of meter.*

Camera   extension tube   lens   filter

2.4

TYPES OF LIGHT METER

Incident light meters

Incident light meters measure the amount of light falling on a subject. A white diffuser first averages the light and a cell beneath the diffuser reads this averaged light. For accurate results, the meter should be placed near to the subject in the same light and pointed toward the camera. The angle at which the meter is held can be critical and should always be pointed directly toward the lens along the same axis. When used in landscape photography, it is often impossible to place the meter close to the subject, which may be some miles off. An alternative method is to hold the meter above your head, facing away from the camera.

The advantage of an incident light meter is that it isn't influenced by highlight and shadow areas in a scene, as a reflected light meter is. On the other hand, because of this, neither can it produce selective exposure information, which proves to be this meter's main downfall, as it removes a layer of creative control.

Reflected light meters

Reflected light meters work in a different way, by assessing the level of light reflected from the subject. Often they are built into the camera and readings are given in the viewfinder. Most modern SLR (single-lens reflex) cameras come with a "through-the-lens" (TTL) meter that measures the amount of light actually entering the lens for greater accuracy.

Reflected light meters are generally more practical than incident light meters because, since they are measuring light reflecting from a subject, there is no need to be in the subject's direct vicinity. With TTL meters, the meter will automatically take into account any light-limiting accessories in use, such as filters or high-magnification lenses.

However, because the reflected light meter will be influenced by both highlights and shadows, as well as mid-toned subjects and everything in between, exposure calculations are often more complex.

In modern cameras, TTL meters provide systems to help overcome this limitation. In the past, basic reflected light meters simply gave a meter reading based on an average of the entire scene. As technology has developed, however, more sophisticated systems have been developed.

2.5

2.6

2.5 & 2.6 *Incident light meters should be pointed directly toward the lens at the same axis for an accurate reading, whereas the reflected light meter can be used at any angle in relation to the lens.*

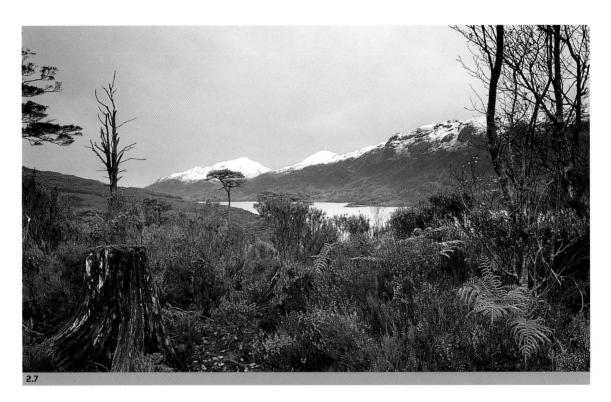

2.7

Multi-segment metering

Multi-segment metering (MSM) is the latest development in metering systems, and can be highly accurate in even the most complex lighting situations. An MSM system takes several independent readings from different areas of the frame and calculates a meter reading based on the findings. In some camera systems, these findings are first compared to a database of "real-life" findings to detect the closest match.

Although MSM has a significant level of sophistication, it works best when metering a scene with a tonal range within the latitude of the film or photo sensor being used, or when there is an even distribution of tones throughout the scene.

Center-weighted metering

Ideal for portrait photography, center-weighted metering (CWM) measures the light across the entire scene but weights the light reading towards the center portion only (usually around 75 percent of the reading is based on a center portion of the frame).

Spot metering

When set to spot metering (SM) mode, the TTL meter takes a reading from a tiny section of the scene—usually an area around just 3—5°. This enables precise metering of specific areas and provides the greatest level of creative control over your exposure settings. SM is an ideal solution when working in high-contrast conditions and where the intensity of light varies considerably throughout the frame.

It is possible to get hand-held reflected light meters that offer a 1° SM facility, which gives even greater accuracy when measuring light in variable conditions. Many landscape photographers prefer to work with a 1° spot meter for this reason.

2.7 *Multi-segment meters are highly accurate and best used where the levels of contrast fall within the latitude of the film or photo sensor.*

2.8 *Center-weighted meters place the emphasis of measurement in a central portion of the frame and are ideal for portraits.*

2.9 *Spot meters allow you to measure tiny portions of brightness in a scene. They are the most accurate meters for high-contrast scenes in which you want to measure just a small portion of the overall frame. They also give the greatest control over the picture-making process.*

2.8

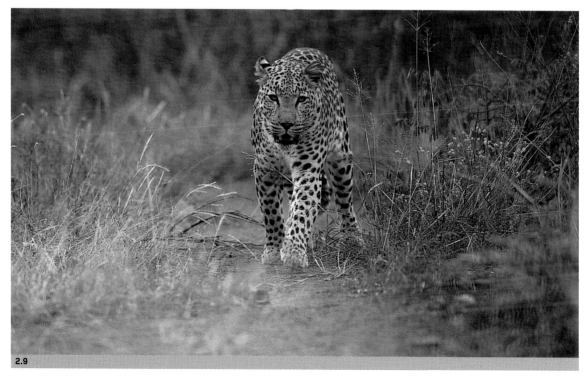

2.9

How a light meter works

All light meters are calibrated to give you an exposure value for a mid-toned subject—that is, a subject that reflects 18 percent of the light falling on it. Examples of mid-toned subjects are leaf green, a clear blue sky at around 11:00am on a summer's day, and London-bus red.

The 18 percent reflectance value is referred to as mid-tone or medium tone because it falls exactly halfway between film's ability to record pure white and pure black. For this reason, it is also referred to as medium gray or 18 percent gray.

I hope this helps you to begin to understand meter readings and their limitations. When you meter a subject, the light meter will give you a reading that will enable you to record it as a mid-toned subject. Now that's fine if the subject you're photographing is mid-toned. But what if it's not? To the meter it doesn't matter because it sees it as mid-toned. But to you it matters enormously because, in most situations, you want to record the subject as it appears. So, having taken the meter reading you must ask yourself the question, "Is the subject mid-toned, darker, or lighter?" If it is darker or lighter than mid-tone, you have to adjust the meter reading that the camera has given you.

Let me give you an example. Say you are photographing a snowman in your garden. You set your camera to auto-TTL metering and take a picture. But, once developed, the snowman looks gray and nothing like the brilliant white you remember. This is because the camera's meter saw it as gray— 18 percent gray to be exact. Now, assume the snowman is still there and take another picture, this time opening up your exposure (adding more light) by two stops. Now when you get your picture developed you will see that the snowman has come out looking exactly as you remembered it: bright, brilliant white. This is because a camera will underexpose light subjects to make them darker and overexpose dark subjects to make them lighter—all the time trying to achieve a tone equal to 18 percent gray. In order to compensate for these exposure calculations you must tell the camera to do the opposite of what it has just done automatically. So, when photographing subjects lighter than mid-tone, where the

2.10

2.11

2.10 & 2.11 *Light meters always give a meter reading that will render your subject a mid-tone. So, when metering white subjects, the camera will underexpose, making your picture too dark. Opening up the suggested exposure setting will rectify this problem.*

camera has under exposed the image, you must tell it to overexpose by dialing in "plus" exposure compensation or by manually opening up the exposure settings. If you are photographing a subject darker than mid-tone, where the camera has overexposed the image, you must tell it to underexpose by dialing in "minus" exposure compensation or by closing down the exposure settings.

While exposure values are often referred to in terms of gray tones, the same rule applies for any color in the visible spectrum. For example, imagine you were photographing a blue sky in the early morning. A direct meter reading would give you an exposure value equivalent to medium blue—a tone of blue you would expect to see at noon. However, in the early

morning the sky will appear much lighter. In order to record it at its true tone, you would need to add more light to your exposure than that indicated by the meter.

2.12

2.13

2.12 & 2.13 *The opposite effect occurs when shooting subjects that are black. When I photographed this black panther, the camera meter overexposed the original image to a mid-tone. Underexposing the camera's suggested setting by a fifth of a stop has achieved a more faithful exposure.*

2.14

2.15

2.14 & 2.15 *While we talk about exposure in terms of gray tones, the same rule applies to color. This photograph taken early in the morning shows a mid-tone blue when taken on auto-exposure. A little compensation (+1 stop) helped to get the exact color that I saw with my eyes.*

2.16—2.18 *These three images illustrate exactly how a photographic light meter will turn everything mid-tone. Originally, 2.16 was black, and 2.17 was white. Only 2.18, an 18 percent gray card, has been reproduced accurately.*

2.19—2.21 *Applying the correct amount of exposure compensation has allowed the camera to reproduce all three colors accurately.*

2.16

2.17

2.18

2.19

2.20

2.21

NOTE

TRY IT FOR YOURSELF

Try this simple test. On an overcast, dry day, place three pieces of card on the ground—one white, one black, and one medium gray. Set the camera's meter to auto-exposure and photograph each piece of card separately, ensuring they fill the entire frame. When you review the results you will see that each photograph appears the same in tone—medium gray. Replicate the test, but this time add two stops of light to the indicated exposure when photographing the white card and take away two stops of light from the indicated reading when photographing the black card. Photograph the gray card at the indicated reading without altering the exposure. When you review this second set of pictures you will notice that each piece of card looks in the picture as it does in real life.

2.30

2.31

Bracketing

However hard you try, and however much care you give to calculating exposure, it is sometimes impossible to get it right. Many factors can influence an exposure, such as very bright sunlight reflecting off shiny surfaces (e.g. water, sand, and glass), constantly changing light conditions, such as those you will encounter on days where broken clouds fill the sky, and subtle variations in a subject's tonality. Something else to bear in mind, and something that is outside of your direct control, is that film manufacturers and processing laboratories operate to tolerance levels that could make a difference of up to a $1/2$ stop in your exposures.

Because of these factors, you may want to bracket your exposures. Bracketing involves taking more than one photograph of the same scene at varying exposure values above and/or below your initial exposure setting. Typically, the variance should be around a $1/3$—$1/2$ stop. On rare occasions, you may want to go as far as +/- 1 stop.

NOTE

DIGITAL CAPTURE

The advent of digital capture has made bracketing less essential because you can instantly replay images. Despite this, bracketing still has a role to play. Consider a scene that involves a fast-moving subject, such as a racing car or a cheetah chasing an antelope. On these occasions, time will not allow for you to check the exposure in the screen and then go back to try the shot again if the resulting image isn't what you had planned. Also, the digital screen on the camera is not always a true reflection of the actual brightness value of the image.

2.32

FLASH METERS

A flash meter works in much the same way as an incident light meter and measures the level of flash light to provide a required lens aperture setting. (In flash photography the shutter speed is usually dictated by the camera, because of the need for synchronization between flash duration and shutter speed.)

The meter is usually held facing toward the camera from the position of the subject. A test flash is then fired to enable the meter reading. Of course, this assumes that you are able to fire a test flash, which often dictates that you are in a studio or using flash under controlled conditions. As with an incident light meter, a flash meter does not automatically take into account any external factors affecting exposure calculation, such as filters or high-magnification lenses.

2.30—2.32 Bracketing an image will help ensure you get an accurate result in difficult lighting conditions. Compare the three images shown here. The first and second images (2.30 and 2.31) show the same image one stop over and one under the original setting. In the final image (2.32), the exposure has faithfully reproduced the original scene.

USEFUL EQUIPMENT

The ability to control and manipulate light for your own purposes is one of the main ingredients for a successful photograph. Of course, this is easier to achieve in a studio with artificial lighting, when you can alter the angle, direction, and size of the light source pretty much at will. Outdoors, it is a little harder to do that with the sun.

Wherever you are photographing, using various photographic accessories can help to persuade light to do what you want in relation to capturing the image you want. However, of the many and varied pieces of equipment out there, which are most useful, and how are they best utilized?

SUPPORTS

Tripods

Tripods are important for vibration-free photography, but particularly so for low-light and night photography, where there is an increased danger of camera shake due to the slow shutter speeds required. They can be a pain to carry but I'd rather have one than not, despite potential discomfort.

There are some key factors to consider when buying a tripod. First, and most important, is rigidity. The sturdiness, of your tripod is determined by two factors: carrying capacity and center of gravity. All tripods are made to carry a certain weight, and they will prove effective up to this weight. Go beyond the recommendation—by attaching a heavier camera—for example, and the tripod becomes less stable. The center of gravity is affected by two factors—the distance between the base and the top of the tripod stem, and the distance between the top of the tripod stem and the top of the camera plate. With both, the laws of physics rule: the lower, the better.

When using a tripod, try to spread your legs wide and even, and always avoid using the center column, if one is fitted. Raising the center column increases the center of gravity and can completely nullify the benefit of using the tripod. If you are using a long lens, attach the lens's tripod collar to the tripod, and not to the camera. An unbalanced camera on a tripod will cause camera movement and, again, reduce the tripod's ability to do its job.

3.1

3.2

3.1 & 3.2 *A tripod is an ideal camera support at any time but particularly in low-light conditions or at night.*

3.3

3.3 *There are all kinds of
tripods and brands of
tripods. If you can, try a few,
to see which suits you best.*

3.4 *When attaching your camera to a tripod, make sure it is well-balanced, using the tripod collar on longer lenses, if necessary, for extra rigidity, and to reduce camera shake.*

3.4

3.5 & 3.6 *I never recommend using the central column of a tripod. Raising it heightens the center of gravity and destabilizes the tripod, reducing its effectiveness.*

3.5

3.6

3.7

Cable releases

I mentioned the cable release earlier and recommend that they are always used in conjunction with a tripod. Modern cameras operate an electronic cable release, which effectively eradicates camera vibration from releasing the shutter. The older-style cable releases (which do actually use a cable) are almost as effective as long as you operate them properly, using a gentle motion on the push mechanism. An alternative solution if you don't have or can't use a cable release is to set your camera to self-timer and press the shutter manually via the main shutter release button, then stand back and let the camera fire the shutter.

3.8

3.7 A tripod is one of the most important accessories in photography.

3.8 When using a tripod, fire the shutter using a remote release.

3.9

Beanbags

I frequently use beanbags when photographing wildlife in low-light conditions. The advantage of the beanbag is that it is far easier to work with in cramped conditions, such as the front seat of a vehicle. When balanced properly, the camera remains quite steady and the beanbag often absorbs any vibrations. On the downside, beanbags do not offer the same degree of sturdiness that a tripod does.

Monopods

A monopod is better than having no support at all, and is helpful for some kinds of photography more than others, notably landscape or other outdoor photography. It is less helpful for low-light and night photography. With the exaggeration of movement caused by multi-second shutter speeds and fast apertures, they are really only slightly better than hand-holding the camera.

Brackets

Brackets can be very useful camera supports, acting in a similar way to a tripod. The key to how successful a bracket will be is what it is actually attached to. If attached to a solid object, such as a thick metal railing, then they will be relatively sturdy and movement-free. However, attached to something less rigid, such as the branch of a tree, or a car window, they are weakened by the very thing that's supporting them.

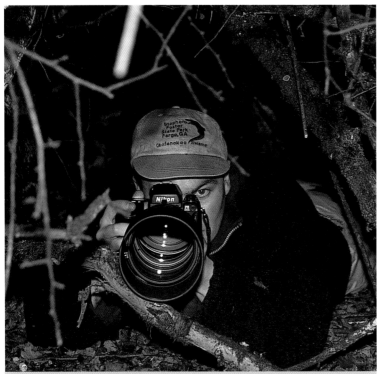

3.10

3.9 *Monopods can be very useful if you are in the field and don't want to carry a tripod.*

3.10 *If you do not have a conventional support, use whatever solid object you can find.*

3.11

3.11 *If you do not have a tripod or monopod with you when out shooting pictures, find a solid support and use a sweater, or similar, to act like a beanbag.*

TIPS

There are some things you can do to minimize camera shake when hand-holding a camera.

First, use your body effectively. Keep your arms tight in to your body and spread your legs evenly. If possible, use a building, fence, or similar structure to support your weight. Make sure that your weight is evenly balanced on both feet. When you are ready to take the picture, take a deep breath and press the shutter release as you are breathing out, as this is when your body is at its most relaxed. Finally, keep breathing, if you can—holding it won't help you achieve a pin-sharp image.

Another option if you don't have a purpose-made camera support is to improvise. A thick woolly sweater on a wall or on your backpack can act just like a beanbag. Once, when photographing out of a kayak, I made a highly effective beanbag out of my life jacket, the foam seating cushion, and a bungee cord. It's amazing what you can find with a little imagination. Another alternative is to find a flat surface, such as the top of a wall, and simply rest your camera on that with the lens supported at the front.

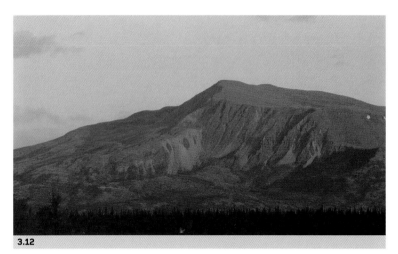

3.12

FILTERS

There are two different types of filter: technical and creative. I am going to concentrate on specific technical filters that are essential to achieve the faithful reproduction of light. Technical filters are those filters that allow you to overcome the limitations of film and photo sensors in recording natural images, or that enhance some of the existing properties of light for artistic expression.

3.13

3.14

3.12 *The original image.*

3.13 *An 81 series filter can add a soft, warm glow to your image.*

3.14 *Don't overdo it—an 81D filter can make your image too orange.*

81 series warm filters

The 81 series of warm filters—so called because they add a subtle orange glow to photographs—are much prized by landscape photographers.

As I related in chapter two, during the day, light varies in color, from deep red to blue-white. All of us have seen photographs of the sunrise and sunset, and the reason for their appeal is their warmth, the so-called "golden hours" of photography.

The 81 series of filters can do one of two things. Firstly, they can help to accentuate the warmth of color at sunrise and sunset. Secondly, they can be used to nullify the blue color cast often visible on film on overcast days or at the height of the summer sun.

Be careful not to overdo things with these filters. Using too strong a tint (81D and above) can give your images an unnatural intensity. Bear in mind, too, that some scenes look better with a slight blue color cast, such as frost, snow, and the twilight hours.

3.15

3.16

3.15 & 3.16 *The original image (3.15) has a blue color cast because of the overcast conditions. The addition of an 81B filter (3.16) gives it a much warmer tone.*

3.17

3.18

3.17 & 3.18 *Adding a blue filter will change the atmosphere of your scene. Compare these two images and see how the different overtones affect your emotional response to the picture. Neither result is right or wrong—simply, different interpretations of a theme.*

3.19 *A neutral density graduated filter will help to even the tones between light areas of a scene, such as skies, and darker areas, giving a contrast that falls within the latitude of the film or photo sensor being used.*

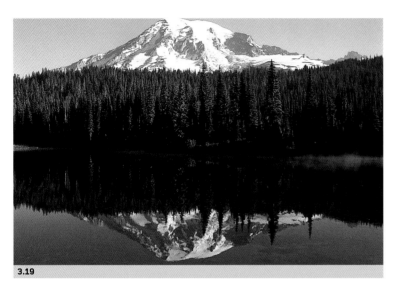
3.19

82 series blue filters

At the other end of the scale, you may need to reduce the extent of warm color casts in your images. This is particularly true when photographing under tungsten lighting with daylight-balanced film, when your images will come out looking overly orange and quite unnatural.

The 82 series of blue filters absorb some of the red waves of light entering through the lens and, in so doing, allow more blue waves to reach and affect the film. The result is a much more natural-looking picture where orange and blue are balanced.

It is possible to use these filters for enhancing blue light in scenes, thereby creating cool, atmospheric images. Applied with skill and to an appropriate subject, this effect can look very dramatic but it takes a little practice.

Neutral density filters

Neutral density (ND) filters come in two sorts (solid and graduated) and various strengths (usually between 1 and 3 stops in $1/2$-stop increments). Solid ND filters are a means of reducing the level of light entering the entire lens. They are useful in

very bright conditions when you need greater flexibility over shutter speed/lens aperture settings. For example, let's say you are trying to blur the motion of water over a waterfall, but the light is too bright to allow a slow enough shutter speed, even at minimum aperture, to create the effect you want. Adding a neutral density filter will reduce the level of light reaching the film/photo sensor, meaning you will need to allow more time—a slower shutter speed—for the correct exposure.

Graduated neutral density filters achieve the same thing, except they only block a portion of light entering the lens, depending on where you position the filter. Typically, ND graduated filters are used in landscape photography where, for example, the sky is far brighter than the foreground. The resulting variation in tone is often too great for the film to handle. Positioning an ND graduated filter, so that the dark section of the filter covers the brighter area of sky, will even out the difference in tones, allowing the contrast to fall within the latitude of the film and producing a photograph with an even balance of tones.

A word of warning when choosing ND filters. The term neutral implies that the filter has no effect on the color of light entering through them. In reality, some manufactured ND filters give a gray cast to light, which is not always pleasing to the eye, though it can enhance stormy skies. It is worth checking this out, if at all possible, before you buy.

Polarizing filters

Another essential for the landscape photographer is the polarizing filter.

Non-polarized light waves exist all around us, for example in light reflected off surfaces, such as water, and in light from blue sky at right angles to sunlight, although our eyes are unable to differentiate between polarized and non-polarized light. Photographic film, on the other hand, records this light causing, for example, reflections on windows, glass, and water.

Polarizing filters polarize the light entering the lens, thus removing these reflections. Another effect is to darken blue skies and make white clouds more prominent. They can be used to good effect on foliage, too, which reflects a lot of non-polarized light, and to intensify the color of glossy objects, such as ceramic and plastics.

Do note that there are two types of polarizing filter: linear and circular. Both affect light in the same way but a linear polarizing filter will affect your camera's auto-exposure function. In order to use TTL-metering, therefore, you will need to use a circular polarizing filter.

3.20

3.21

3.20 & 3.21 *Adding a polarizing filter can saturate colors, such as a blue sky, which, in this instance, helps to accentuate the clouds.*

USING POLARIZING FILTERS

1 Polarizing filters have the most effect when the camera is at 90° to the sun.

2 Before taking the picture, rotate the filter through 360° to observe what level of polarization gives the best results.

3 Circular polarizing filters work best with auto-focus, auto-exposure system cameras.

4 If manually calculating exposure values use the following as a guide to compensation values:

$1/4$ polarization	$+ 1/2$-stop
$1/2$ polarization	$+ 1$-stop
$3/4$ polarization	$+ 11/2$-stop
Full polarization	$+ 2$-stops

5 Use a polarizing filter for full-bodied colors, such as reds and blues.

6 Polarizing filters will remove unwanted surface reflections from water and moisture, as well as the reflections from surfaces such as glass.

Ultraviolet (UV) filters

Ultraviolet light is invisible to the human eye but not to camera film. The effects of UV light on film can be an increase in blue color cast and haziness in the atmosphere. It is most apparent in shots taken at high altitude or close to the coast. A UV filter reduces UV light entering the lens, enabling images to appear on film as they do to the eye.

UV filters are often sold with camera lenses as standard, partly because they can be kept on at all times and double-up as protection for the front element of the lens. I use them only when necessary, because they are an extra barrier for light to travel through, which reduces the quality of light reaching the film.

A similar filter is the skylight filter. Skylight, or haze filters, do the same job as UV filters except that they have a pink tint that reduces the blue color cast.

3.22

3.23

3.24

3.25

3.22 *Light is a form of electromagnetic radiation that vibrates in a plane at right angles to the direction of travel. A plane polarizer allows only light vibrating in one direction to pass through.*

3.23 *A polarizer has the strongest effect when angled at 53° to the vertical —known as the Brewster angle—and when the angle between the reflected and refracted beams is 90°.*

3.24 & 3.25 *Here, a polarizing filter removes some of the unwanted glare reflecting from the closed car window.*

LENS HOODS

Light enters the lens at different angles, and the larger the diameter of the lens the greater the angle of entry. These stray angles of light can cause lens flare—which you may have seen on TV and on some of your pictures—small, hexagonal marks increasing in size from the light source.

In moving films, flare can add to the atmospheric presence of a scene, but in still photography they are simply distracting. Using a lens hood fitted to the front of your lens will help keep lens flare to a minimum and improve the quality of your pictures.

It is important to match the lens hood with the lens, because some lenses—particularly wide-angle lenses—can cause vignetting.

3.31

3.32

3.31 & 3.32 *When shooting into the sun, stray light can reflect off the various elements in the lens and cause lens flare (3.31). Adding a lens hood will help to solve the problem (3.32).*

3.33

3.34

REFLECTORS

There are two types of reflector: panel and lighting attachments. In this section I am referring only to panel reflectors, how they work and when to use them.

The purpose of a reflector is to balance light and moderate the areas of shadow. In that way, they act very much like a fill-light, throwing light into parts of the scene unlit by the main light source. The beauty of the reflector is that it can never be brighter than the source light, which means a reflector will complement your lighting and not overpower it.

3.33—3.35 Panel reflectors throw light back into the subject's shadow areas, helping to balance and moderate tones. 3.34 shows a model shot without a reflector. Notice how the addition of a reflector in 3.35 changes the level of contrast between light and shade.

3.35

Positioning

The purpose of a panel reflector is to bounce light back into the shadow areas on the subject. As such, they are usually positioned directly opposite the main light source and close to the subject. The beauty of a panel reflector is that they can never be as bright as the primary light source and, therefore, they will retain some shadow, which maintains depth and definition.

Surfaces and color

While a reflector can be any color, they generally come in four colors— white, silver, gold, and blended. There is also a black reflector. The color of the reflector influences the color of the light reflected back onto the subject. Which color you decide to use depends on your desired effect.

3.36

3.37

3.36 *White reflectors tend to have a more even distribution of light and are neutral in color tone. Light from a white reflector also tends to be softer than light from metallic-colored reflectors as it is more diffused.*

3.37 *If you look at a silver surface, you will notice that it is made up of light and dark areas. The smoother the surface the less pronounced the contrast. Silver reflectors make the reflected light more directional than the light obtained from a white reflector, with an accompanying increase in contrast.*

Black reflectors

The purpose of a black reflector is not to reflect light but to absorb it. In soft lighting conditions, such as an overcast day or when using a soft box in a studio, shadows are softened with less well-defined edges. While this can be a preference, there may be occasions when you want hard, contrasting shadows in your picture. A black reflector will help to add contrast into a picture by absorbing the stray light that occurs with diffused lighting conditions.

3.38 *The same effect is achieved with a gold reflector, though the color balance is warmer because of the yellow/ orange undertones. While the warmth can be pleasing in some situations, it can be overbearing in others, particularly indoor portraits. For that reason, gold reflectors are more likely to be used outdoors.*

3.39 *A blended reflector is made up of a combination of gold and silver. The effect is a cross between the two, giving more natural-looking warmth to portraits than a straight gold reflector. This makes them a better alternative for indoor portraits, where the subtler color cast will complement rather than overpower the subject.*

3.40

Sizes

Reflectors come in many different sizes, from the small ones that easily fit into an average gadget bag, to the very large that will just about fit into a studio. But, in photography lighting terms, the true size is the reflector's total area relative to the size of the subject. For example, place a small reflector (30cm/12in) next to a dragonfly and it becomes a large reflector. Similarly, place a large reflector (150cm/60in) next to a building, say, and it becomes a small reflector. So, when deciding on the size of reflector to use, you must first consider the size of the subject you are photographing.

Another issue to consider relating to size is portability, particularly when using a reflector outdoors. Many of the larger reflectors today come as fold-up packages, where the reflector can be folded down to a third of its normal size. This makes transportation much easier.

3.41

3.40 *Some reflectors, such as this model produced by Lastolite, come with built-in handles for easy holding.*

3.41 *In the studio it is possible to get special brackets for positioning and holding reflectors.*

TIP

Remember that a light-colored wall can be used as a reflector if the subject is positioned correctly.

Handling reflectors

The biggest challenge when using reflectors is holding and supporting them in the right place. (Of course, if you've got an assistant, this isn't an issue.)

In the studio, you can get purpose-built stands that have a clamp facility to hold the reflector in position. Outdoors is a bigger challenge. If you are photographing beyond arm's length from the subject, then find a suitable object to lean the reflector against, such as a wall. If you are within reach of the subject then you could just try holding the reflector by hand. Some reflectors now come with a built-in grip to make this easier. If you are going to hand-hold, I recommend using a cable release or remote shutter release for extra mobility.

The weather conditions play a part outdoors. In windy conditions, large reflectors have a tendency to take flight if not secured in some way. Carry some string or fishing line to attach the reflector to the support you're using.

That said, I can't emphasize how much better persuading a friend or family member to join you outdoors can be. You just need to find one crazy enough for the job!

NOTE

MAKING YOUR OWN REFLECTOR

You can make a reflector relatively easily or, indeed, improvise with material you can find around the home.

A reflector is simply a piece of highly reflective opaque material. White nylon is ideal and, if attached to a frame made from garden cane, or a piece of dowling, for example, will create a perfectly acceptable reflector. This also has the advantage that it will act as a diffuser if placed between the light source and the subject. A piece of white art board works equally well, as would a thick sheet of expanded polystyrene.

To make a metallic reflector, first take a piece of silver or gold aluminum foil, and crumple it up in your hands. Unfold the crumpled sheet and glue it over a piece of thick card or hardboard, sealing it at the back with some tape.

3.42

3.44

3.43

3.45

3.42—3.45
It's easy to make your own panel reflector.

3.46

3.47

DIFFUSERS

If you are shooting in direct lighting conditions, you may want to diffuse the light source to soften the shadows and reduce contrast. A diffuser goes between the light source and the subject, and changes a point source to an omni-directional source by scattering the light. This is exactly the same as what happens when clouds obscure the light from the sun.

A diffuser is generally made from white nylon (although any transparent material will work). If the material is colored then the diffused light will also be colored. For best results, the material should allow around 50 percent of the light to pass through it.

There are other accessories that you can use to add to your creativity and effective use of light. Many of these, such as honeycomb grids, umbrellas, and barn doors are covered in the section on studio lighting (page 178). Of the others I may not have mentioned, my advice is simple: experiment. Most lighting techniques and effects are learned in this way, and you will understand lighting best when you see for yourself how small changes you make result in very different images.

3.46 & 3.47 *A direct point light source can be diffused to create omni-directional lighting. Even outside in direct sunlight, a diffuser will help to reduce levels of contrast, which may not enhance the scene.*

NATURAL LIGHT

If you photograph in a studio with artificial light then you have complete control over the lighting conditions. Changing the angle of light, its direction relative to your subject, and even its color, is a relatively simple process. However, outdoors—or in a daylight studio—you lose much of this flexibility and you have to work with what nature provides.

For many photographers, natural light has an inner beauty that artificial light simply can't match. It is like a living being with a character and personality that it imposes on the landscape. And, like any living being, the mood of light changes depending on circumstance. Time of day, the changing seasons, and weather all play their part in the fickle nature of light, and directly impact on the emotional story of your photograph.

4.1

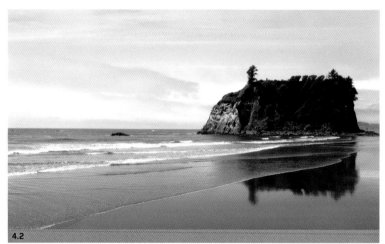

4.2

LIVING WITH LIGHT

To literally see light, and to interpret how subtle changes in the quality of light alter our perception of a scene, is one of the things that sets the professional apart from the amateur photographer. Being able to use natural light effectively, altering your circumstances to suit the picture—rather than altering the lighting as you would in a studio—will determine your ability to gain maximum visual impact and heighten the viewer's emotional response to your images.

First, you must understand how time and weather alters the light. As you develop your instincts to interpret the fluctuations in the quality of light you will find that your ability to *predict* photographs, rather than *react* to happenstance, increases the compelling visual power of your images—that special "wow" factor.

4.1—4.3 *As the angle of the sun changes, so does the color of light, from warm orange in the early morning (4.1), through yellow during mid-morning (4.2), and blue at the height of the day (4.3).*

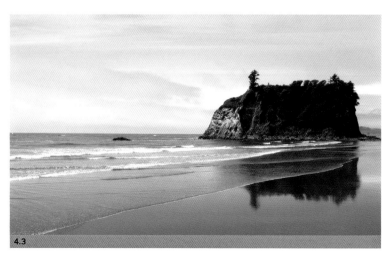

4.3

4.4 *As the angle of the sun relative to the earth's surface increases, so the color temperature of light increases. When the sun is at a low angle the color temperature is low. At the sun's peak, around midday, the color temperature is at its highest and light appears white.*

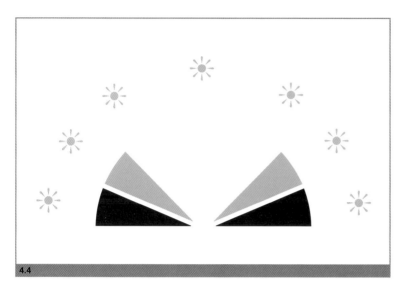

4.4

FROM DAWN TO DUSK: LIGHTING THROUGH THE DAY

As the sun moves across the sky, two things occur that affect your photography. First, the angle of the sun in relation to your subject changes—from low angle at sunrise and sunset to high-angle at midday. The angle of the sun dictates the depth of shadows, which, in turn, emphasizes different components of the picture. A low angle produces long shadows that accentuate shape and texture, while a high angle minimizes shadows, reduces the illusion of depth, and gives flat lighting that emphasizes surface features.

As the angle of the sun increases, the temperature of the light changes, and with it the color of light. These changes influence the mood of the scene with the deep oranges of early morning and late evening. As the angle of the sun increases and, with it, the level of white light entering the scene, so the color temperature alters, giving a blue color cast that makes your images appear cooler. How strong this blue color cast becomes depends on determining factors, such as cloud cover.

So, under natural lighting conditions, how your subject is lit is dependent on the time of day you photograph it. Timing may well also determine the type of film or white balance settings you use, or whether you use accessories such as color correction filters or reflectors.

4.5

4.5 *In the early morning and in late afternoon when the angle of the sun is low, shadows are long. As the sun rises during the day the length of shadows decreases and is virtually non-existent when the sun is directly overhead.*

4.6

4.7

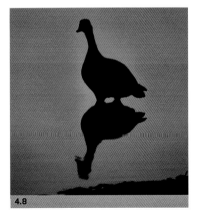
4.8

Sunrise

Many landscape photographers
consider sunrise to be the ideal time
of day for photography. This partiality
to early morning light is not only
because the light is often rich in
warm colors and the shadows
emphasize shape and texture,
but also because morning light is
cleaner and more crisp due to the
lack of dust in the air that can be
caused by the high levels of human
activity during the course of the day.

4.6 *Early sunrise over the
rocks at Dunstanburgh,
Northumberland, England.*

4.7 *The soft light of sunrise
penetrates the early
morning mist near Durdle
Door in Dorset, England.*

4.8 *This lighting in this shot,
taken at sunrise, shows the
powerful, graphic effects
you can achieve.*

4.9

Early morning

As the sun rises, additional white light penetrates the earth's atmosphere and the deep red and orange of sunrise succumbs to a brighter, more yellow light. But, the long, form-filling shadows remain, making early morning a favorite time for landscape photographers.

4.11

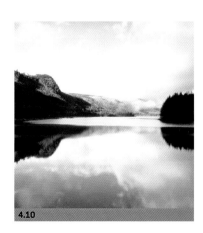

4.10

4.9 *Early morning is an ideal time to photograph still landscapes such as this scene of Mirror Lake in New Zealand.*

4.10 *This shot nicely captures the tranquillity of an early morning lake scene.*

4.11 *The Jurassic coast in Dorset, England. Early morning haze can add a surreal quality to landscapes.*

4.12

4.12 *Aira Force, Lake District, in England.*

Late morning

By late morning, most of the warm color is lost as a higher level of white light now penetrates the atmosphere. Shadows, too, begin to shorten, with the result that texture detail and form begins to fade. As shadow depletes so does contrast. The effect can be liberating (or not) depending on what you are trying to achieve with the picture. For example, contrast and shadow when the sun is at a low angle intensifies form, but that same lighting can also hide important detail.

4.13

4.14

4.13 *A coastal resort, Cornwall, England.*

4.14 *A stone church in Northumberland, England.*

Midday

At midday the sun is at its peak and at the highest angle to the ground. You will often hear the light at midday referred to as "flat", because the lack of shadows created by the high angle of the sun reduces the illusion of depth in a photograph. This lack of shadow, however, can be used to your advantage when photographing subjects where the main emphasis is placed on the features of that subject, such as record shots of buildings.

4.15

4.16

TIP

Because the lighting conditions of afternoon mirror that of the morning, the same enhancement and compensation factors apply. The principal difference, of course, is that the shadows cast will run in the opposite direction to the morning, and you must decide prior to the day's shooting which direction of shadows lend the best composition.

4.15 *The "southern Alps",
South Island, New Zealand.*

4.16 *Urquhart Castle on
Loch Ness, Scotland.*

Afternoon

Once the sun has reached its peak, it begins its descent toward sunset. The shooting conditions during the afternoon mirror that of the morning: the color temperature begins to reduce and a yellow glow replaces the harsh white light of noon. As the day draws on, the late afternoon light takes on a deeper golden glow and shadows begin to reappear, creating the illusion of depth and giving form and texture to subjects.

4.17

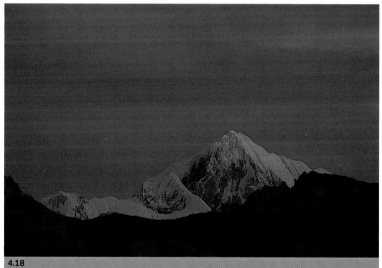

4.18

4.17 *Greymouth, South
Island, New Zealand.*

4.18 *Lenticular cloud over
Mount Tasman, South Island,
New Zealand.*

Sunset

Sunsets are one of the most popular
photographic subjects. Like sunrise,
the light at sunset is full of deep,
warm colors and the shadows cast
by the low angle of the sun are soft
and long. Shapes take on a three-
dimensional form as the contrast
between lit and unlit areas of the
scene intensifies.

You often find that the oranges and
reds of sunset are deeper than those
of sunrise. This is not because the
color temperature is any different
but because of the level of dust in
the air. At sunrise, the earth is settled
from the night's relative inactivity.
During the day, we create dust that
lingers in the air which is constantly
disturbed by activity. This dust affects
the way light is reflected and helps
to create the appearance of more
intense colors.

4.19

4.19 *Seattle skyline, Washington, USA.*

Dawn and dusk

Dawn and dusk are periods in between light; the time when day and night merge. It is the period when darkness fades and daylight threatens, and an ethereal atmosphere pervades. During this time, light doesn't last very long, but offers the photographer some of the most beautiful conditions in which to photograph, where the colors are warm yet subtle, and where the shadows have soft edges.

Photography at dawn and dusk also gives you the opportunity to mix natural and non-natural light. For example, in the image above (4.19), the darkening sky highlights the huge variety of artificial lights in the cityscape.

TIP

One of the things you'll notice most about low light is that it doesn't last very long, which means you must work quickly, ideally having pre-chosen your shooting position, or at least given yourself enough time to decide on your composition and set up your camera. You will also be shooting at long exposures and will need to consider the law of reciprocity failure.

4.20

4.21

4.22

FROM SUN TO STORM: LIGHTING AND THE WEATHER

Everything I have discussed thus far has assumed consistent weather conditions. Of course weather changes, and with it the lighting conditions in which you photograph. For example, the intensity of light on a cloudless day is much greater than it is when storm clouds fill the sky. Depending on the weather, the sun can change from a point source—like a spotlight—to an omni-directional source where the lighting is spread around more evenly, similar to a photographic light box. And, a misty morning can give light an almost ethereal character.

Thus, in much as the same way as the time of day changes the angle of light and the color temperature of light, the weather also affects the temperature and the size of the light source. And, as the time of day affects the mood of your photographs, so too will the weather conditions.

4.20—4.22 *The weather conditions will affect both the size of the light source and the mood of your pictures. Compare these three images and see how the different conditions create different emotional responses.*

4.23 *On cloudless days, when the sun is directly overhead, images can appear flat and lacking in form.*

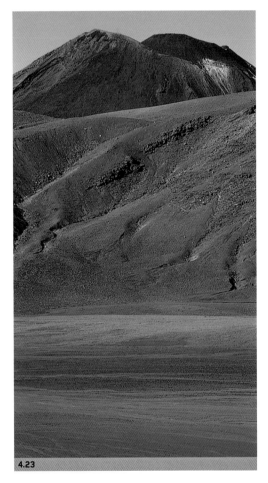

4.23

Clear blue skies and sunshine

Most people, when they talk about "good weather", are referring to the sort of weather we see on bright, sunny, cloudless days; the sort of weather we all want to experience on vacation.

Photographers, however, are different. For us, bright cloudless days are some of the worst days for photography: featureless skies, harsh shadows, and high contrast produce dull scenes and thorny technical problems.

The key to making the most of direct sunlight is to combine it with the most sympathetic time of day and turn some of its limitations to your advantage. For example, direct sunlight often causes high levels of contrast. Turning this contrast to your favor and shooting when the sun is at a low angle in the sky can produce some very effective silhouettes. Altering the exposure settings and exposing for the foreground will completely alter the effect and produce "rim" lighting, lending your subject a beautiful "halo".

So, by combining direct sunlight with a low angle and shooting into the light, you can create stunning, evocative images full of visual energy and powerful personal expression.

4.24

4.24 *The rays of light in this image create a soft, dreamy atmosphere.*

4.25—4.27 *Waiting until later in the day means you can use the point source of light from the sun to create more artistic and appealing effects, such as silhouettes, and rim lighting.*

4.25

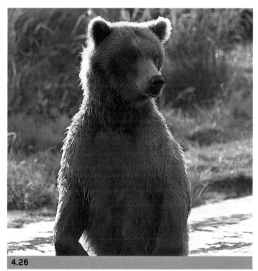

4.26

TIPS

Try to avoid vast expanses of blue featureless sky by dropping the angle of the camera and raising the position of the horizon, or by including tall structures, such as buildings or trees, to break up the skyline and add interest.

Use the high levels of contrast to your advantage by shooting into the light early in the morning or later in the afternoon, creating silhouettes and golden halos around your subject.

When shooting into the light, be careful not to look directly at the sun, and use a lens hood to help avoid lens flare.

Avoid high, overhead direct lighting when photographing portraits outside.

4.27

4.28

4.29

4.28 & 4.29 *Broken cloud helps to bring interest to otherwise featureless skies.*

4.30 *Ever-changing lighting conditions, which can be caused by broken cloud passing in front of the sun at irregular intervals, can make setting exposures a complicated affair.*

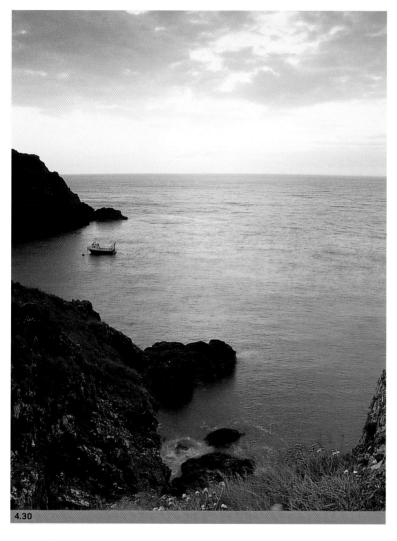

4.30

Broken cloud

Sunny days do not always have clear blue skies, but are often accompanied by large, white fluffy clouds. Broken cloud offers the photographer two advantages. Firstly, it helps to break up featureless blue skies, adding interest to landscape pictures. Cloud formations are often a prerequisite if selling images to postcard publishers, for example. Secondly, when a cloud drifts in front of the sun, it acts as a large diffuser, turning direct sunlight from a point source to an omni-directional source of uniform light.

This even spread of lighting softens shadows and reduces contrast, giving a much less harsh feel to the scene, and producing sympathetic lighting for outdoor portraits. However, one of the problems of broken cloud is that because the intensity of light is always changing, metering for exposure becomes a continuous activity throughout your shooting time.

4.31

Overcast days

On overcast days, the cloud cover acts as a giant diffuser throwing a completely uniform level of light on the scene below. It is the same effect as attaching a diffuser box to the front of a flash unit. This uniformity softens shadows and reduces contrast to a greater degree than broken cloud conditions and is ideal for photographing subjects that suffer under these conditions, such as portraits and waterfalls. Similarly, intensity of light fluctuates far less, making calculating exposure a simpler task.

A downside to overcast days is that, like clear blue skies, overcast skies lack any real interest for the landscape photographer. Even their color, white or gray, is uninteresting. So, when photographing on overcast days, it is just as important to reduce the area of sky visible in the picture by changing the angle of the camera or using tall structures, such as trees, to add interest.

4.31 & 4.32 *Overcast conditions, where the clouds turn the direct sunlight to an omni-directional light source, can be ideal for photographing scenes such as waterfalls, forest streams, and leafy glades, which demand subtlety.*

4.32

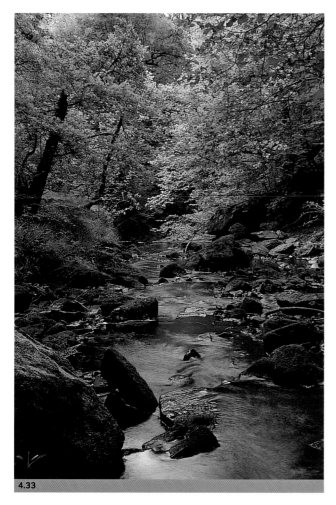

4.33 *The light in this image is diffused by the shade of the trees, but, combined with the overcast light, it makes for an atmospheric shot of this glade.*

4.34

4.34 *When photographing high-contrast scenes, such as this Brown bear fishing for salmon at the waterfall along Katmai River, direct sunlight can make a well-balanced exposure impossible. Waiting until the sky is overcast will reduce levels of contrast and give more even tonality.*

4.35 *The problem with overcast days is the lack of any subject interest in the sky, which can be a problem for landscape photographers.*

4.33

TIPS

SHOOTING ON OVERCAST DAYS

Use the reduced level of contrast and soft shadows to photograph subjects that are suited to these conditions, such as people, flowers, woodlands, and waterfalls.

Restrict the area of sky visible in the picture by changing the angle of the camera, using a longer focal length lens to narrow the angle of view, or by using features to add interest.

4.35

Stormy weather

While the thought of racing out into a storm with all your electronic equipment and instrumentation is daunting, if not a little foolish, stormy weather can be the inspiration for highly evocative, characterful images that transform an average scene into one of high photographic impact—the "wow" factor, again.

Storm conditions can provide some of the most dramatic lighting effects in outdoor photography. From landscapes where dark, ominous skies are counteracted by brightly lit foregrounds, to shafts of light cutting through breaks in the clouds, through to one of everyone's favorite natural phenomena: rainbows.

The difficulty of photographing in stormy weather—aside from the practical problems—is due to variations in the intensity of light across the scene. While these variations create interesting and strong compositions they need to be metered for carefully, and minute adjustments made to compensate for the variations. Sometimes, these adjustments can only be made in the darkroom or on the computer at the processing stage. However, post-camera processing can be minimized by effective use of compensating filters, such as neutral density graduated filters that help to equalize variations in tone.

4.36—4.39 *Venturing out in stormy weather may not be your idea of fun. But, for the dedicated photographer, stormy conditions can produce some of the most compelling lighting conditions imaginable— from rainbows to multiple lighting effects.*

4.36

4.37

4.38

4.39

TIPS

Keep your camera protected from the elements.

When confronted with variations in light intensity, make a decision on which part of the scene is the most critical to your composition and meter for that spot.

Use graduated neutral density filters to help equalize the tones between dark skies and brightly lit foregrounds.

Adjusting your camera position can increase the intensity of color in rainbows.

Use the differences in light intensity to add to the dramatic atmosphere of the scene.

4.49

4.50

4.51

4.49—4.51 *Fall is a time of
beautiful rich, warm colors,
which can be exploited by
the outdoor photographer.*

Fall

Fall is the season of color, and
these colors can be used in your
compositions to beautiful effect.
It is a powerful communicator, and
mixing the reds of dying leaves with
the greens of mosses and evergreen
trees will give your pictures a special
visual energy. To bring out the texture
and detail in fall foliage, the best time
of the day for photography is mid-
morning and mid-afternoon. Like
springtime, sunrise is later in the
morning and sunset earlier in the day.
And, like springtime, the sun doesn't
rise fully overhead, which is ideal for
landscape photography.

TIPS

Photograph leaves and foliage
during mid-morning or late
afternoon in order to catch the
best light for emphasizing texture.

Fall colors can be given
added saturation by using a
polarizing filter.

Use directional light to
emphasize the rich colors of fall
and try compositions that match
complementary colors, such as red
and green, to give your pictures
visual energy.

4.52

4.53

4.54

Winter

Winter is one of my favorite seasons for photography. The low angle of the sun, the extra clarity of the light, and the lack of foliage all move toward emphasizing the elements of design—line, pattern, shape, and texture—that are the cornerstone of making photographs.

Winter days are short and sunsets are early. However, it is possible to do some good shooting throughout the day due to the low angle of the sun, with its accompanying long, form-filling shadows.

In winter, colors tend to be muted—pastel shades are more prominent than the deep, saturated colors of summer and fall. This effect can be pleasing, giving your images a subtle ambience, but if extra saturation is required, then using a polarizing filter will help to bring out existing color.

4.52 *In winter, the angle of the sun often remains low throughout the day, providing great opportunities for special lighting effects, such as the backlighting on these ice crystals.*

4.53 *Winter is a wonderful season for photography where graphic elements of design, such as line and pattern can be exploited for strong photographic compositions.*

4.54 *The low angle of the sun also produces strong shadows, which help to accentuate form and give pictures a three dimensional feel.*

TIPS

Use a polarizing filter to bring out colors that are muted over the winter period.

Make the most of the low angle of the sun by shooting throughout the day.

Use the lack of dense foliage to emphasize the graphic elements of your composition.

WHEN TO PHOTOGRAPH WHAT

The following is a guide to the best conditions for photographing particular subjects. That is not to say that these are the *only* times at which to take pictures of those subjects, but simply ideas, or prompts, for those times and conditions that are proven to work for your photography. For example, if I suggest photographing cityscapes in winter, it doesn't mean they can't be photographed at any other time of the year.

One tip I give to students at my workshops is to experiment. Never be afraid to try ideas "outside the box". For example, when photographing moving subjects, rather than using a fast shutter speed to freeze motion, try shooting at 1/4sec, say, and see what happens. By way of another example: many advise never to shoot portraits outdoors at noon on a clear summer day because of the unflattering shadows created by direct midday lighting. Yet Edward Weston, one of photography's greatest exponents, once shot a

whole portfolio of portraits in this way with great success. So, experiment with your own ideas. How you see and interpret different lighting conditions is all part of developing your own photographic signature. And, after all, the only person who will see any unsuccessful results is you. In the meantime, here are some ideas for you to play with.

Subject	Time of day	Weather	Season	Comment
Tree silhouettes	Sunset	Clear	Winter	The lack of leaves on trees in winter adds to the design element of the picture, emphasizing line, which is further enhanced by the strong graphic statement made by silhouettes.
Portraits	Early morning or late afternoon	Overcast	Any	Overcast lighting will soften the shadows and reduce contrast. Use a reflector to lighten the shadow side of the subject.
Wildlife	Early morning or late afternoon	Clear	Spring/ summer	Wildlife activity is greater in spring and summer. The warm glow of early morning and late afternoon sun will add to your composition.
Coast	Sunrise	Clear	Any	Warm light at sunrise can often be complemented by sea mists, lending pictures a beautiful radiance.
Postcard scenes	Late morning or early afternoon	Broken cloud	Summer	Postcard publishers prefer pictures to have bright, fluffy clouds and sunny weather.
Woodland/forest	Early-to-late morning and late afternoon	Overcast	Fall	The fall colors of woodlands and forests are one of photography's highlights. Overcast weather will help to reduce contrast, while low-angled sunlight brings out the texture in leaves. For added color saturation, use a polarizing filter.
Waterfalls	Morning or afternoon	Overcast	Winter/ spring	Waterfalls are notoriously high in contrast subjects and are best photographed in overcast conditions, which reduce contrast. Higher rainfall in winter and spring adds to the level of water flow. Some waterfalls can dry up in summer and fall.

Subject	Time of day	Weather	Season	Comment
Flowers (close up)	Early morning or late afternoon	Hazy	Spring/ summer	Use the low angle of early morning or late afternoon sun to bring out the texture in petals. Overcast conditions reduce contrast but you may want to add a polarizing filter to saturate the colors.
Flowers (expanses)	Late morning or early afternoon	Clear, broken cloud, overcast	Spring/ summer	Large expanses of flowers often look best when set off against a clear blue sky.
Mountains	Sunrise and early morning, late afternoon to sunset	Clear or broken cloud	Any	Mountains look good at all times of year, often blanketed in snow during winter and a backdrop to flowering meadows in summer. Low-angled light will help to give them a three-dimensional form.
Hills and valleys	Early morning or late afternoon	Clear	Any	The low angle of light in early morning and late afternoon helps to give hills and valleys form.
Lakes	Early morning	Clear (and still)	Spring/ summer	On very still sunny days, the surface of a lake can produce mirror-like reflections.
Rivers	Sunrise and early morning, late afternoon, sunset	Clear or broken clouds	Any	Silhouetting the bends in the river against a colorful sunrise or sunset can produce a distinctive graphic statement.
Cityscapes	Dusk or night	Any	Winter	Reduced levels of dust in winter gives a clarity to the scene that can be obscured by smog or haze in summer. Waiting until dusk or nightfall will bring the city to life with a mix of natural and artificial light.
Still life	Early morning or late afternoon	Overcast	Any	Shadows formed by low-angled sunlight will give form to still-life subjects, while reduced contrast from overcast weather will make faithful exposures easier.
Snow	Early morning or late afternoon	Clear	Winter	Backlighting on a clear winter's day will bring out the best in snow and ice crystals.
Record shots	Midday	Overcast	Any	The midday sunlight will reduce shadows and emphasize the features of your subject.
Insects	Early morning	Hazy	Spring/ summer	Insects are best photographed when it's cooler, since low temperatures make them inactive. Clear mornings are always cooler because cloud cover works as an insulator, retaining heat at the earth's surface.
Pets	Early-to-late morning and late afternoon	Overcast	Any	The slightly brighter light of late morning and early afternoon will enable you to select faster shutter speeds to freeze movement. Overcast conditions will help to soften shadows and reduce contrast.
Fast-moving action	Late morning and early afternoon	Clear or overcast	Spring/ summer	Fast-moving action often requires the use of fast shutter speeds. Brighter weather conditions will allow you greater flexibility in your exposure settings.

4.55

CHANGING LIGHT

Sometimes, even waiting just a single hour can make all the difference to the type of light illuminating the landscape. Study the pairs of photographs, here and overleaf, and see how changing light has completely altered the mood of the images.

The first image of Banburgh Castle, in Northumberland, England, (4.55), was taken at around 5pm on a fall day. The sky is still blue, which, combined with the dark rocky foreground, gives the picture a cool, mysterious feel. The low angle of the sun creates shadows on the castle walls, giving the castle a three-dimensional form. In the second picture, (4.56), taken about an hour later at around 6pm, the mood has completely changed. The setting sun bathes the scene in a warm pink glow. A slow shutter speed has given the incoming sea a ghostly effect, which, together with the pastel coloring, makes for a calming picture. Notice how, with the sun below the horizon, the dark shadows on the castle walls, evident in 4.55, have become much softer and have almost disappeared completely, giving the castle a flatter appearance.

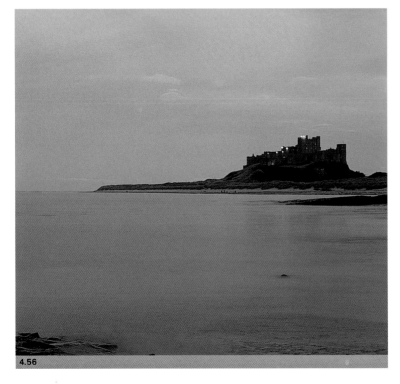

4.56

4.55 & 4.56 *Banburgh Castle, Northumberland, England.*

4.57

4.58

A similar effect occurs with these images taken in the Okefenokee National Wildlife Refuge in Georgia, USA. The first image, (4.57), taken at around 4:45pm as the sun begins to set, still has an overall blue cast, giving the scene a much cooler atmosphere. In the second image, (4.58), taken 30 minutes later, the sun has set and the picture comes alive with deep shades of yellow, orange, and pink. Notice, however, how the image is less calm than the sunset taken at Banburgh Castle, where the pastel colors soften the overall image. Changing the format of the image to vertical, (4.59), changes the emphasis of the picture, and another, (4.60), 30 minutes later, at dusk, the colors change again, creating a more moody image.

4.59

4.60

4.57—4.60 *Okefenokee National Wildlife Refuge, Georgia, USA.*

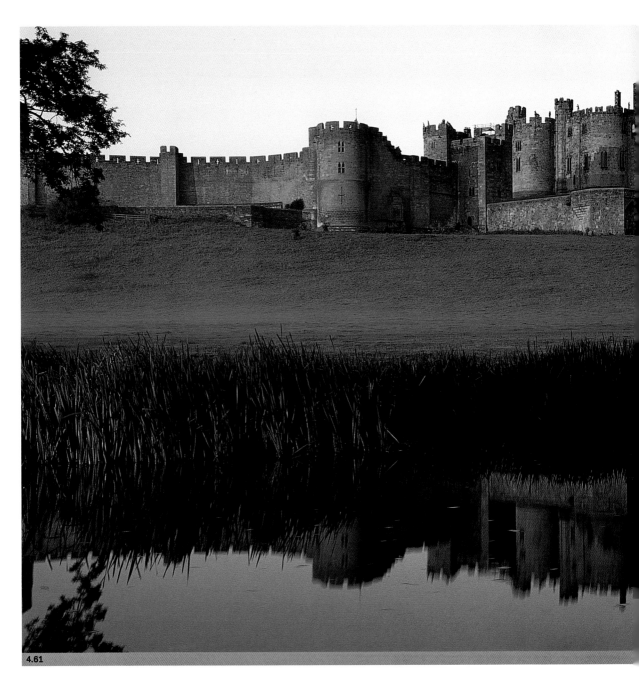

4.61

4.61 & 4.62 *Alnwick Castle, England. Light affects the way a photograph is perceived, and should be a major consideration when thinking about composition.*

4.62

The same change in mood and color temperature can be seen in the early hours of the morning. In these images of Alnwick Castle in Northumberland, England, the difference in appearance of the castle between the first shot, taken at 8am (4.61), and the second shot (4.62), taken just an hour later, is a stark one. Sunrise was late in the morning as these pictures were taken in late fall. The color temperature in the first image is very orange, giving the picture, and the castle walls in particular, a beautiful warm glow. In the second picture, at around 9am, the warmth has subsided considerably and a much cooler image is created. Notice, too, how the low angle of the sun in the first picture adds a high level of contrast to the bank of reeds at the edge of the river, giving them form and depth. An hour later, those same reeds appear much less interesting, as the contrast is lost.

4.63

4.64

DIRECTION OF LIGHT

Changing the direction of light in
relation to your subject will alter
the level of texture and detail in the
picture. Again, study the pairs of
images over this, and the next few
pages, to see how the direction of
light affects the final image.

Side lighting

In both these images, the early
morning sun, at a low angle to the
subject, has cast shadows—in 4.63 to
reveal the undulating surfaces of the
snow, and, in 4.64, along the length
of the reed. These shadows have
given both of the subjects form
and a three-dimensional image on a
two-dimensional surface—the film.
If taken much later in the day, both
images would have appeared flat
and uninteresting, and it would have
been impossible to see the texture
in either.

4.63 *Frans Joseph Glacier, South
Island, New Zealand.*

4.64 *Lake Matheson,
South Island, New Zealand.*

4.65

Top lighting

Top lighting, such as that found around midday when the sun is overhead, produces very flat images, lacking in shadow and, therefore, contrast. In the image of the Grand Canyon in Arizona, USA (4.65), this works well as it helps to detail the sedimentary layers in the rock face. However, the picture lacks depth and it is difficult to distinguish between one wall of rock and another. Some depth is given by including the cacti in the foreground. Notice the difference, however, between the appearance of the rocks in the left of the image and those in the top right of the picture, where shadow has formed—the rock takes on a much more three-dimensional look.

In the second image, of Monterey in California, USA (4.66), again, there is a complete lack of depth in the picture due to the absence of shadow. It is difficult to tell how far apart the boulders in the foreground are from the central rock and, in turn, from the boats in the background. However, it is easy to pick out features throughout the picture, which provides the kind of subject information that is often sought by postcard and calendar publishers.

4.65 *Grand Canyon, Arizona, USA.*

4.66 *Monterey, California, USA.*

Backlighting

Backlighting can be used to great creative effect, producing silhouettes and rim-lighting and helping to isolate and emphasize some of the elements of design fundamental to making good pictures.

In the first image, (4.67), backlighting has been used to create a contrast between the warm fall colors of the leaves and the multi-directional line of the tree branches. Neither side-lighting nor top lighting would have created this highly graphic effect.

The second image, (4.68), is less graphic, and places more emphasis on mood. Taken in Yosemite National Park in California, USA, backlighting has been used to emphasize the cloud creeping into the picture in the top right corner of the image. If this picture had been taken from the opposite direction, it would have produced a very flat image with little or no interest for the viewer. The effect is to create a picture with a slight sense of foreboding.

4.67

4.67 *Westonbirt Arboretum, Gloucestershire, England.*

4.68 *Yosemite National Park, California, USA.*

4.73

4.73 *Mount Cook and Mount Tasman, South Island, New Zealand.*

4.74 *Yosemite National Park, California, USA.*

4.75 *Tongariro National Park, North Island, New Zealand.*

4.74

4.75

4.76

Clouds as subjects

A problem with cloudless skies is that plain blue can look a bit dull, and lacking in substance. Clouds add interest to your composition.

In the image taken at Yosemite National Park, California (4.74), the sky is completely clear and, while it doesn't overwhelm the picture, neither does it add any real interest.

Another image, (4.75), photographed in the volcanic mountains in Tongariro National Park in New Zealand is far more interesting. The wisps of clouds creeping into the picture space in the top right corner of the frame add interest and a sense of depth.

Sometimes, clouds can be the subjects themselves. The images of Greymouth in New Zealand, (4.76 and 4.77), were taken late in the day. The contrast in color, which creates layers in the image from top to bottom,

gives a sense of depth, and the altering shape of the clouds creates a visual energy. It is also an illustration of how the density of cloud cover affects the level of light passing through the cloud.

4.76 & 4.77 *Greymouth, South Island, New Zealand.*

4.77

LOW–LIGHT AND NIGHT PHOTOGRAPHY

Many photographers head indoors when the sun goes down, but those who do are missing out. Low-light and night photography offer the photographer great opportunities for creative image-making. From the sky at night to the landscape at dusk and dawn, from cityscapes to wildlife—the scope for your camera is huge. What puts many off is having to learn new techniques, but the fundamental principles of photography at night are the same as those during the day. The rules of composition are the same, and light is still the essence of the captured image. So, what are these "fearsome" new techniques that make us prisoners to daylight? This chapter will help you find out.

GETTING STARTED WITH LOW–LIGHT AND NIGHT PHOTOGRAPHY

The basic fundamentals of photography are no different in low-light and night photography, but there are some techniques that are more prevalent, which are worth mastering. Principally, you will be working with slow shutter speeds and fast apertures, making blur from camera shake and vibration a real enemy. Calculating exposure will be more difficult to ascertain, and focusing can become a major challenge.

As well as some of the specifics mentioned below, it is sensible to make sure you are fully aware of how your camera operates—the position of the relevant controls, the direction of turn on dials for setting shutter speed and aperture, etc.—before you venture out. While I advise this for all types of photography, it is especially useful in the dark, since you won't have the same visual reference as that available during the day. Knowing how to operate your camera "blind" can save a lot of time, and sometimes will make the difference between getting the shot or not.

ESSENTIAL GEAR

The belief that low-light and night photography requires lots of new, expensive equipment is a bit misleading. Yes, you will require some additional kit, but none of it is particularly expensive and you may already have some of it.

Cameras

The main requirement of a camera in low-light conditions is that the shutter must be left open for long periods of time. At the very least this means that your camera must have a shutter-speed setting referred to as the "Bulb" setting. When set to "Bulb" the shutter will remain open for as long as the shutter release remains depressed, which can be for seconds, minutes, hours—and even days! Many modern SLR cameras have shutter-speed settings up to several seconds in regular increments (1, 2, 4, 8, 16, 32) and this can make long exposures slightly more accurate. Though, to be honest, the difference of a second or two during a 30-second exposure is minimal.

Another useful, though non-essential, tool built into some cameras is a facility for altering your film speed setting manually. This allows you to "push" your films—to make them work at a faster ISO rating than they are calibrated for. With digital cameras, this facility is replaced by an ISO equivalency setting, which allows you to alter the sensitivity of the photo sensor for each shot, and it is much more flexible than pushing film.

A very useful tool when using SLR cameras is the mirror lock-up facility. Most of the vibration incurred when releasing the shutter is caused by the action of the mirror flipping up out of the way of the shutter curtain, allowing the light to pass through to the film/photo sensor. By locking-up the mirror prior to firing the shutter, the vibration is eradicated. This facility tends to come with only the more expensive SLR cameras. Some mid-range digital cameras offer the same facility, although, while more versatile, are often slightly less effective.

With film cameras, the mirror is locked-up manually before the shutter is released. This has the advantage of removing all vibration caused by the mirror flipping out of the way of the shutter curtain, but does mean that you lose vision through the viewfinder and you also lose auto-focus and auto-exposure capabilities. This may be less of a problem in very low light where neither function operates effectively anyway. With digital cameras, the mirror is electronically locked-up after the shutter is depressed, but before the shutter curtain is opened. This allows you a constant view through the viewfinder and continued operation of auto-focus and auto-exposure up to the point of release. However, there is then a delay in the shutter curtain opening, which may cause you to miss the shot, for instance, if your subject is moving. It may also mean that you get some vibration. As with most things in photography, it's a bit of a compromise!

The last thing your camera must have is either a cable-release socket and/or a self-timer. When shooting in low light, it is important to minimize camera vibration. This can be diminished if a cable release or self-timer function is operated.

5.1 *To capture a scene in fading light at the end of the day, you will need a tripod, and must set your exposure to "Bulb".*

5.2

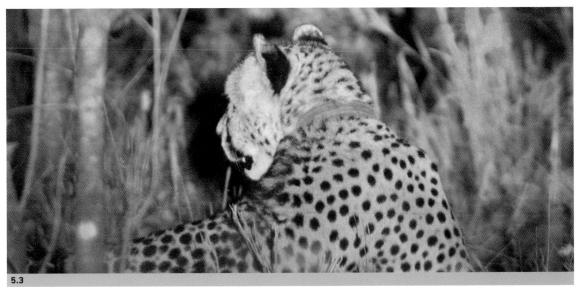

5.3

5.2 & 5.3 *With SLR cameras the speed of the lens will determine the brightness of the image in the viewfinder. When a lens is attached to a TTL camera it automatically opens up to its widest aperture, irrespective of the actual setting used in any given shot. Therefore, a lens with a fast (wide) aperture will allow in more light making the scene brighter than a lens with a slower aperture.*

Lenses

The lenses used for daylight photography are also suitable for low-light conditions. What is important to consider is the speed of the lens. A fast lens, such as a lens with an aperture of f/2.8 or faster, has two advantages over a slower lens (f4 or slower). Firstly, it allows you extra stops of light. For example, a lens with a maximum aperture of f/2.8 is two stops quicker than a lens with a maximum aperture of f/5.6—

allowing four times as much light to reach the film/photo sensor at the same shutter speed. This has the advantage of letting you use faster shutter speeds, even when light levels are low. The second main advantage is the brightness of the viewfinder (for an SLR camera) and the ease with which you can see your composition and set your focus distance. A lens with a maximum aperture of f/2.8 allows additional light through the lens, making it is easier to see what

you are doing in the viewfinder. This is not an issue with rangefinder cameras, and it is worth checking the level of brightness of the viewfinder if you are using this type of camera.

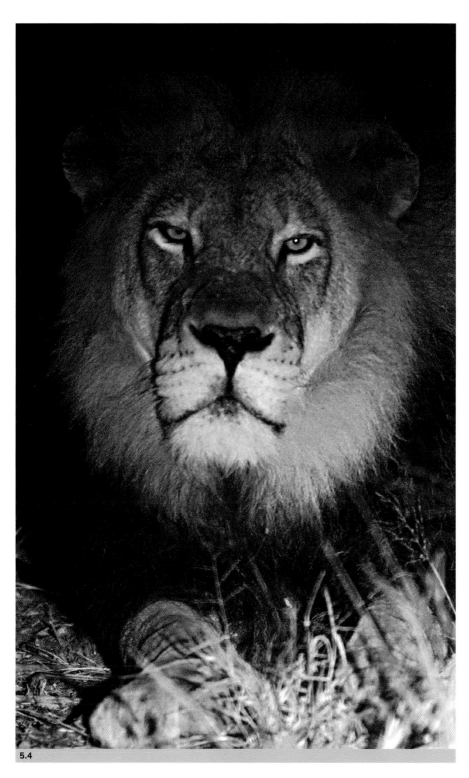

5.4

5.4 *To capture this image, I required a lens with a fast (wide) aperture to allow as much light as possible into the shot.*

5.13

5.14

5.15

FLASH AND METERS

Flash units

If you are shooting at night and in low light, you may well want to use flash as the primary light source for fill lighting. The type of flash unit you need is dependent on what you are shooting, but your major consideration should be the guide number, which determines the power output of the flashlight.

Hand-held exposure meter

While your camera may have a built-in flash meter, such as a TTL meter, it may be limited in low-light conditions. Firstly, it may not operate at the levels of light you're working in, when exposure values may be outside the range of your meter. Secondly, the lighting conditions may be quite complex, requiring you to make minute measurements of individual areas to calculate an accurate exposure. In these cases, your camera will need a spot meter and, if it comes without one, invest in a hand-held meter.

In very low-light conditions, hand-held incident light meters (or combination incident/reflected light meters) have an added advantage if the white dome (invercone) is removable. The white dome on an incident light meter averages the light falling on it to give an 18 percent mid-tone value. It does this by allowing only 18 percent of the light falling on it to reach the metering cell below. If you remove the invercone, all the light falling on the cell will be read. Effectively, this makes the cell five times more sensitive to light, giving a light reading in conditions that would be impossible with the cone attached. Of course, you'll need to make the necessary adjustment to the reading given; multiply by 18 percent—or 20 percent to make life a little easier—to obtain the correct exposure value, or reading.

5.13 Portable flash unit.

5.14 Hand-held reflected light meter.

5.15 Combination reflected light meter and incident light meter.

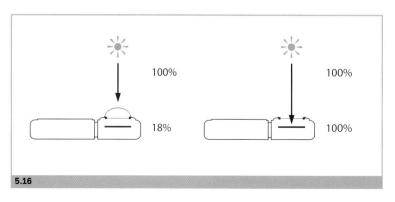

5.16

100%

18%

100%

100%

5.16 The invercone, or simply, cone, on an incident light meter absorbs 82 percent of light falling on it to give a mid-tone reading. Taking it off allows 100 percent of light to fall on the meter, which can be useful for calculating exposure in low-light photography.

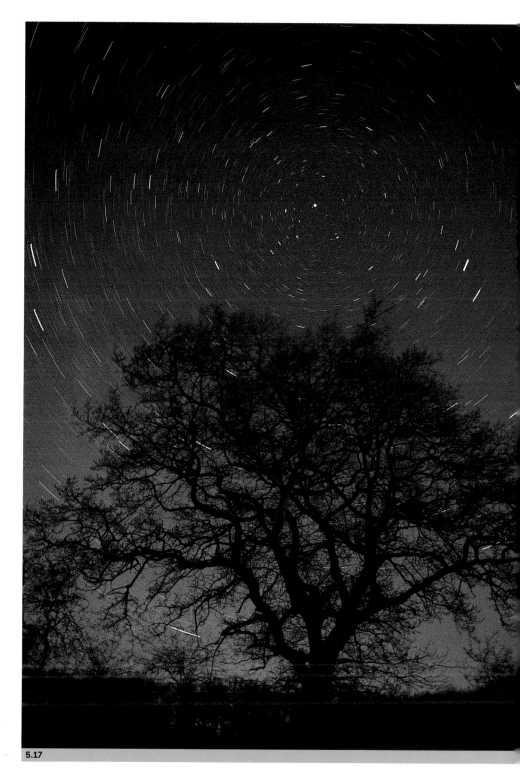

5.17 When taking shots of the sky at night, set your shutter speed to "Bulb" for a few hours in order to achieve blurry stars. It's a great way to show time in motion.

5.17

High-contrast scenes

It is quite feasible that you will be photographing scenes where low levels of natural light are complemented by bright artificial light. A typical example is a cityscape at night where the black sky and dark streets are enlivened by the glow of lights left on overnight, floodlit buildings, street lamps, and car headlights. In such a complex scene as this, exposure calculation becomes difficult because of the varying levels of illumination and the stark contrast between an almost black sky and the brilliance of the lights.

Given this type of situation, you must decide what effect you are trying to achieve with your photograph and expose accordingly. That is, exposing for the highlights or for the shadows. In this example, if you exposed for the highlights, then the shadows would be severely underexposed with the result that they'd appear black in the photograph. On the other hand, if you exposed for the shadows, then the highlights would be grossly overexposed and would appear washed out. As a general rule, it is better to have detail in the highlights than in the shadows.

Subject	Recommended aperture/ shutter speed at ISO (ISO equivalency) 400	Compensation for reciprocity failure: 400 ISO slide film
Floodlit buildings at night – front on to camera	1/4 sec @ f/4	None
Floodlit buildings at night— angled to camera	1 sec @ f/8	+ 1/3 stop
Funfairs (to freeze motion)	1/125th @ f/2.8	None
Funfairs (to blur motion)	1/15th @ f/8	None
Fireworks	Up to 1 min @ f/8 or f/11	None
Lightning	Up to several min @ f/8 or f/11	None
Star motion	4—8 hours @ f/8	None
Moon (clear night)	1/250th @ f/16	None
Floodlit sports events (to freeze motion)	1/125th @ f/5.6	None
Floodlit sports events (to blur motion)	1/30th @ f/11	None
Car-light streaks (busy road)	10—20 sec @ f/22	None
Landscapes (under full moon)	4 min @ f/11	+ 1.5 stop
Landscapes (under partial moon)	8 min @ f/11	+ 1.5 stop
Street scenes (with sidewalk lights)	1/4 sec @ f/8	None
Cityscapes (close up)	2 sec @ f/11	+ 1 stop
Cityscapes (wide-angle)	8 sec @ f/11	+ 1 stop

5.23 *St Catherine's, Dorset, England.*

5.24 *Bourbon Street, New Orleans, USA.*

5.25 *Night scene, Tokyo, Japan.*

5.26 *The Great Clock housing "Big Ben", Westminster, London, England.*

5.23

5.24

5.25

5.26

5.27

Long exposures and the laws of reciprocity

I have alluded to the laws of reciprocity failure. The principle behind it relates to film's sensitivity to light. Under usual photographic operating conditions (i.e. shutter speeds measured in fractions of seconds), the laws of physics determine that a change in one exposure control (lens aperture or shutter speed) can be compensated for by an equal and opposite change (a reciprocal change) in the other. That is, an exposure setting of 125th sec at f/11, for example, allows exactly the same amount of light to reach the film/photo sensor as an exposure setting of 1/250th sec at f/8; 1/500th sec at f/5.6; 1/1000th sec at f/4, and so on. Of course, the rule also applies in reverse. For example, 1/60th sec at f/16; 1/30th sec at f/22, etc. This balance works without fail until you enter the realms of long-time exposures, which are generally considered to be greater than one second. When exposing film for long periods, film's sensitivity to light suffers some fall-off, and this causes the laws of reciprocity (equal and opposite changes) to fail. In effect, the longer film is exposed to light, the less sensitive to light it becomes. Thus, when photographing at long exposures, you need to add some additional light, to make up the balance. The question, of course, is exactly how much compensation is required? Unfortunately, there is no simple answer to that question. While, in theory, the laws of reciprocity failure are an exact science, in practical terms they are not. The level of compensation needed will depend on not only the length of time the film is exposed to the light, but also on the emulsion used. Different film types (e.g. transparency film, negative film, black and white film) react in different ways, and different makes of film within the same grouping (e.g. Fuji Velvia, Fuji Provia, Kodak Ektachrome, Kodachrome) also react in contrasting ways.

5.27 At night, when shutter speeds are measured in seconds, rather than fractions of seconds, you need to allow for reciprocity law failure. Here, I added an additional stop of light to my calculated exposure in order to get a faithful reproduction of the scene.

FUJI	1sec.	4sec.	16sec.	64sec.
Fuji Velvia (RVP)	None	+ 1/3rd stop	+ 2/3rd stop	Not advised
Fuji Provia 100F (RDP III)	None	None	None	None
Fuji Astia 100 (RAP)	None	None	None	+ 1/3rd stop
Fuji Provia 400F (RHP III)	None	None	None	+ 2/3rd stop
Fuji Sensia 100 (RA)	None	None	none	+ 2/3rd stop
Fuji Sensia 200 (RM)	None	None	None	+ 2/3rd stop

KODAK	1sec.	10sec.	100sec.
Ektachrome E100VS (Pro)	None	None	None
Ektachrome E100SW (pro)	None	None	Not advised
Kodachrome 64	Not advised	Not advised	Not advised
Kodachrome 200	+ 1/2 stop	Not advised	Not advised
ELITE chrome 400 (EL)	1/3rd— 1/2 stop	1/2 stop	Not advised
PORTRA (Pro) 160NC/ 160VC/400NC/ 400VC/400UC	None	None	Not advised
SUPRA (Pro) 100/ 400/800	Not advised	Not advised	Not advised

The table, above, gives some indication of the compensation required for some films on the market today, as recommended by the manufacturer. As with all things photographic, I suggest you use these figures as guidelines only and run your own tests to evaluate the effects of reciprocity failure for your own photography.

NOTE

A TEST FOR RECIPROCITY FAILURE

1 Find an even-toned scene or subject to photograph.

2 Set up your camera on a tripod in low-light conditions.

3 Calculate your exposure in the usual way, and apply an exposure setting where the shutter speed is 1/2sec, with the lens aperture as close to fully open as possible. (If this isn't possible, wait until the level of light has decreased.)

4 Take a photograph at this setting. This is your base picture against which you can compare the following set of images.

5 Now take several more pictures, lengthening the shutter speed each time (e.g. 1sec, 2sec, 4sec, 8sec, 16sec, and so on) and making the reciprocal change in lens aperture.

For example, if your base setting is 1/2sec at f/4, your following exposures should be 1sec at f/5.6, 2sec at f/8, 4sec at f/11, 8sec at f/16, 16sec at f/22, etc.)

6 Bracket each shot +1/3rd stop, +2/3rd stop and +1 stop.

7 Have the film processed and review the results. You should see an increasing level of underexposure as the shutter speeds reduce on the non-bracketed images. Now review the bracketed images and decide what level of compensation gives the best results at the given shutter speed for the film used. If you use different film types, you will need to test each individually.

5.28

5.29

Long exposures and digital noise

The laws of reciprocity failure do not affect digital photo sensors in the same way they affect film. However, long exposures with digital capture cause another effect to occur—digital noise.

Digital noise occurs because of the electro-magnetic properties of the photo sensor, and appears as unrelated and adjacent pixels. On your digital photographs, noise has a similar appearance to the grain of film. And, as with grain, the bigger the enlargement of the original image, the more perceptible the noise becomes.

At fast shutter speeds, the proportion of noise relative to image pixels is very small and therefore not obvious. However, the longer the photo sensor is active (i.e. exposed to light), then the greater the proportion of noise to image pixels and the more obvious it becomes.

Some digital cameras come with a "Noise Reduction" option specifically for use in long exposures and I would highly recommend using it when your shutter speeds exceed one second.

5.30

5.28—5.30 *Digital photo sensors do not show grain in the way film does but, instead, is affected by digital "noise", which looks much like grain. These images show the effect of digital "noise" before noise reduction is applied and after.*

5.31 *Shooting into the fading light of day on a very slow shutter speed, and using a tripod, produces this stunning silhouette.*

TIPS

NIGHT AND LOW-LIGHT PHOTOGRAPHY

1 The essential gear for night and low-light photography are a tripod and remote shutter release.

2 When calculating exposure, remember to compensate for reciprocity law failure.

3 Fast ISO-rated films/digital photo sensors react more quickly to light but increase the proportion of grain/noise.

4 Take time before shooting to allow your eyes to get accustomed to the dark.

5 Hand-held light meters are often more sensitive to light, and thus work better in low-light conditions.

6 Because of the limitations of auto-focus systems, it is often easier to focus the scene manually.

7 On a practical note, take care when out alone at night, and, preferably, take someone along to accompany you.

CLOSE-UP AND MACRO LIGHTING

One of the main advantages of macrophotography is its ability to reveal detail in subjects that are often too small for the human eye to see clearly. Sure, we can see a bumblebee drinking nectar from a flower, or a dragonfly hovering over a pond or stream, but, it is not until you get very close that you can begin to pick out the intricate detail.

Good lighting plays a significant part in creating truly outstanding photographs in close-up situations. The challenges, however, are numerous, not least of which is finding a light source large enough and close enough to give maximum depth of field, while minimizing hard shadows and light fall-off.

6.1

EXPLOITING ARTIFICIAL LIGHT

While natural daylight can be used in close-up and macrophotography, it is a specialty that lends itself ideally to artificial light. Some photographers are critical of this, citing unnatural overtones, hard shadows, and black, featureless backgrounds as evidence. And, while all of these factors can occur, each can be overcome by careful selection of flash position and subject-to-background separation.

Working with a single flash

While most photographers using flash seek out the most powerful unit available to them, the close-up and macrophotographer has another perspective. For them, a small, low-powered flash unit, close to the subject becomes a broad, large source of light similar to daylight on an overcast day or a large studio flash bounced off an umbrella.

It is true that flash photography in close-up and macro work takes some experimentation, particularly if you are working with a non-TTL flash unit. When photographing with a manual unit, you will need to try some test shots, moving the flash unit around to ascertain the best position for your particular brand and model. However, once you have identified the most suitable position, then this set-up will produce consistent results for most subjects. The exceptions will be when photographing very bright or very

dark subjects, when you will need to make some minor adjustments. (Minus 1-stop or so for white or highly reflective subjects, and plus between $1/2$—1-stop for dark subjects.)

With auto-TTL flash, the process is far simpler as the flash unit will, in theory, modify the output of the flash to suit the situation. In practice, however, I would still recommend running some tests, since the likelihood is that the auto-system will slightly overexpose the scene. This is mainly due to the fact that while the control chip will respond in billionths of a second, the flash cannot turn itself on and off quickly enough, and some excess light will spill onto the scene.

6.2

NOTE

TESTING FLASH–TO–SUBJECT DISTANCE

These tests are easy to fulfil by following these simple steps:

1 Set your camera on a tripod, or other secure support, with the flash unit attached and angled at around 45° to the subject.

2 Make a set of exposures at f/8, f/11, f/16, and f/22. These will form your base exposures.

3 Examine the images. If they are all too bright, then move the flash further away, maintaining the angle at 45°. If they are all too dark move the flash unit closer, again, maintaining the 45° angle.

By trial and error, identify the best exposure at f/16 and make a note of the flash–to–subject distance, with the flash angled at 45°. This will form your standard shooting position with flash.

6.1 & 6.2 *Black backgrounds occur because of the rapid fall-off of light from smaller flash units. They can be visually striking, as shown here, but are not to every photographer's taste.*

6.7

Highly reflective surfaces

Surfaces with a high reflectance can produce hot spots when photographed with flash. To prevent these hot spots from overpowering your composition, use a diffuser over the flash head(s). This will soften the quality of light and mute any overly bright areas of the image.

Twin highlights

When using a twin-flash set up, and sometimes when mixing natural and artificial light, it's common to record twin highlights in the eyes of insects and other creatures. These look unnatural because we are used to a single highlight (the earth having only one sun). There is not much you can do to avoid this effect, other than a single flash unit when appropriate.

6.8

6.7 & 6.8 *Highly reflective surfaces can produce hot spots when photographed with flash.*

6.9 *Twin highlights in the eyes of insects and animals can be difficult to overcome when using a twin flash.*

Continuous source lighting

So far I have talked mainly about flash lighting, but continuous source lighting, such as tungsten and fluorescent lighting, is another possibility for you to consider. One of the main advantages of continuous source lighting is that you can see the effect of the lighting on your composition before you make the photograph. This enables you to identify hot spots or hard shadows and adjust your lighting accordingly.

One potentially major disadvantage with tungsten lighting for close-up work is the heat tungsten lamps give off. Because tungsten light is relatively low-powered, it needs to be placed close to the subject for the best results. However, get too close for any length of time and the tiny creature you are taking care of will fry.

USING NATURAL LIGHT

When shooting close up outdoors, natural light may be your preferred option. The quality, direction, and color of natural daylight will all impact your pictures and either enhance or detract from the overall effect.

For most close-up subjects, hazy, diffused light is ideal with the lower levels of contrast, helping to retain detail in highlights and shadows. Mid-morning, when the sun is at an angle of around 45°, the direction of the light will help to create shadows on textured surfaces that will add form to your composition. However, if the light is too direct then you may find the shadows too harsh and it would be better to wait until the sun disappears behind a cloud.

If the natural light conditions prove far from perfect (and let's face it, this is photography we're talking about so we know that's going to happen), then carrying a small reflector with you may help to save the day. In close-up and macrophotography, reflectors (even small ones), can play a vital role. Placed close to the subject, they can soften shadows and alter the direction of the light falling on your subject. On bright sunny days, you can use them as a shield to diffuse the light falling on your subject.

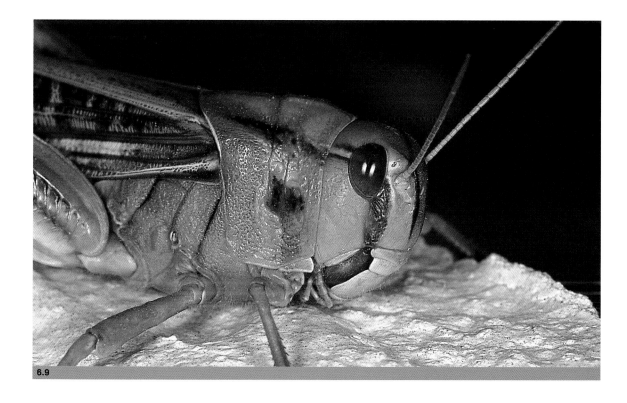

6.9

THE DAYLIGHT STUDIO

When you think of studio photography, you tend to think of intricate, artificial lighting systems. Often, of course, this is the case but there are times when you can use natural daylight to great effect in the studio.

The advantage of using natural light for indoor photography is that the light, having been reflected off multiple surfaces, is usually soft, subtle, and muted, making it ideal for portraits with a gentle or romantic atmosphere. Shadows are very low key, and contrast is minimal. As usual, there is a downside. Often, the level of light will be very low, necessitating slower shutter speeds and faster apertures, increasing the likelihood of motion blur and reducing depth of field.

We all accept, however, that the art of photography is about meeting constant challenges, and the daylight studio is a great place to begin learning the fundamental techniques of studio photography.

SETTING UP A DAYLIGHT STUDIO

Choosing a room to work in

This may sound like an obvious statement to make, but anyone who has ever commandeered the family bathroom for a darkroom will know where I'm coming from: before you plunge headfirst into setting up a daylight studio at home, first consult anyone else with access to the room to gauge how long you'll have it to yourself. This is particularly important if you're working with a model, since constant interruptions will soon disrupt the flow of your photography.

The next thing to do is to select a room that is large enough to work in (look for high ceilings and open floor space), with plenty of sources of natural light. This could mean having two, or more, windows on different walls, or a window and outside door. Multiple light sources are not essential but will give you added flexibility when posing or setting your subject. If you have only a single light source to work with, such as a single window, try to use a room with a large window to give you more options.

Rooms as props

For some styles of photography, you may prefer to work with some props. These help give your pictures a sense of place and will dictate the room you work in. For example, if photographing mothers with babies, you may use a nursery as the setting. In glamor photography, a bathroom or bedroom may be a suitable location to set up, or to depict a craftsman at work, a workshop is an appropriate venue.

Making up the room for photography

Once you have decided on the room, you will need to make sure it's a practical location for photography. Try to keep the floor space clear of clutter and make sure there is a natural walkway around immovable objects. Using the source of light as your guide, select the areas you will set, or pose your model and then imagine photographing her/him there. Look through your viewfinder and check to see what the background looks like. Are there any obtrusive elements that will detract from your photograph? If so, move them. Unless they are part of your pre-visualized plan, remove pictures from the walls and make sure that any nails or holes that are left won't appear in the picture. Anything that doesn't add to the composition of the picture should be taken away and kept out of sight.

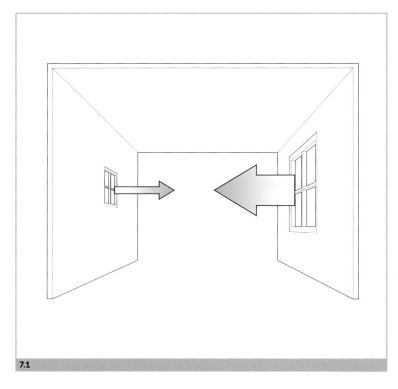

7.1

7.1 *Having more than one light source, preferably from large, south-facing windows, will enable you to light your subject more effectively.*

Setting up a daylight studio | Choosing a room to work in
Rooms as props | Making up the room for photography | Sources of light

145

Sources of light

Obviously, the most important element of your daylight studio is your light source. Usually, this source will come from one or more of three different areas: windows, doorways, or skylights. Doorways and windows will generally give you side lighting, which is ideal for rendering form and texture, and is typically more pleasing to the eye.

Windows are often better placed than doorways and provide more usable light, though this isn't always the case. For instance, patio doors can provide a large amount of light.

Skylights are ideal for replicating the lighting found during the middle of the day. On a cloudy day, much like a small window or narrow doorway, they can turn an omni-directional source of light into a point source. They are also ideal when mixing natural light with fill-in flash, since the flash is less noticeable, giving you more natural-looking effects.

I assume that you are unable to change the position of the light source, and so this will dictate how you set or pose your model. You can, however, change some aspects of the source, such as its size (and quality), direction in relation to the subject, and its color.

7.2

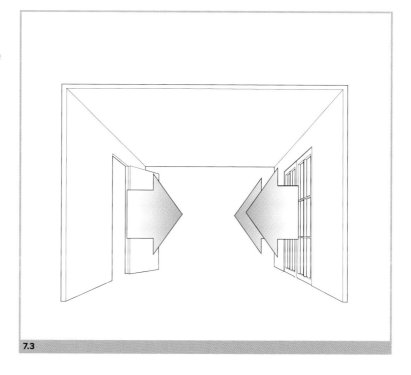

7.3

7.2 *Skylights will enable you to light your photography from above.*

7.3 *Doorways and windows are ideal sources for side lighting.*

7.4

7.4 *The light from the window is the only source of lighting in this shot, but even without a diffuser to "scatter" the light, the effect is simple and pleasing.*

7.5 *Most of the time, you may only have a single light source, a window, to light your daylight studio, so it is worth finding ways to enhance the effects.*

Size of lighting

Let's say you are using a single window as your light source, and that the window is a fairly standard size—around 150 x 120cm (59 x 47in). You can increase the effective size of the window (light source) by putting a diffuser over the glass, which will further scatter the light entering from outside.

Alternatively, you can decrease the effective size of the window (light source) by blacking out a section of it, creating a more direct point source. And, just as with daylight outdoors or in an artificially lit studio, the size of the light source will affect the quality of light, either soft and low in contrast, or hard and high in contrast.

7.5

7.6 *Here, a diffuser was made to fit over the glass to "scatter" the light.*

7.6

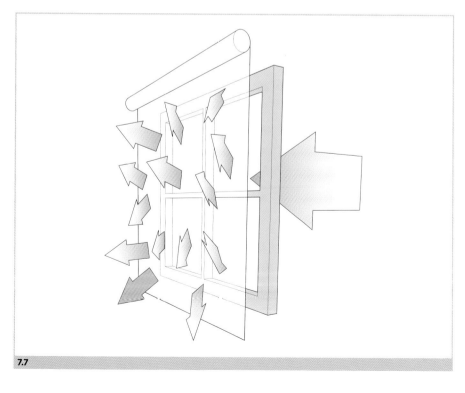

7.7 *"Scatter" your light by introducing a diffuser to enhance the lighting on your subject.*

7.7

Direction of light

While you can't change the actual direction of the light, you can change the position of the subject in relation to the light. Position your subject at a right angle to the window and you have side lighting, giving your subject form and highlighting texture detail. Turn your subject 90°, and you have backlighting, producing silhouettes, or rim lighting. If your room has a skylight then you can recreate overhead daylight conditions, which may be useful if you are trying to photograph a subject's features rather than its form or texture.

Color of light

By placing a colored diffuser between the light source and your subject, you can change the color of light. For example, let's say that it's the middle of the day but you want an effect more like that of sunrise or sunset. By placing a yellow or orange diffuser over the window and positioning your subject at 90° to the source, you will achieve the effect you're after.

Other daylight studio locations

You don't necessarily have to utilize your own home for your daylight studio. Other options are available, if not always as convenient. For example, old barns make ideal daylight studios, as well as providing a natural prop for some kinds of photography, particularly glamor. If you can, make use of any easily hired space that offers good natural light.

7.8 *When setting up your lights around your subject, consider the direction of the light to suit the portrait, and whether you want to use a diffuser to add some soft color to the shot.*

7.8

7.9

7.9—7.11 *This sequence of images demonstrate the ways in which your subject can be lit naturally, with the help of simple accessories, such as a color diffuser, to create different effects.*

NOTE

ESSENTIAL KIT FOR THE DAYLIGHT STUDIO

There are some things I wouldn't be without when shooting in a daylight studio. Reflectors will hugely increase your lighting options, allowing you to add fill light into areas that would otherwise be in shadow. For similar reasons, I would also carry a diffuser—even if this equated to a large white bed sheet—in order to increase the size of the light source. I would also advise setting the camera on a tripod, which will give you more options with shutter speed and, by default, give you greater control over depth of field.

7.10

7.11

7.12

Fill-in flash

Mixing natural light and artificial light is not unusual, whether photographing indoors or outdoors. The purpose of fill-in flash is much the same as the purpose of using a reflector. Fill-in flash adds illumination into shadow areas of the scene and helps to reduce contrast.

When using fill-in flash, it is important that you get the exposure right. One of the advantages of flash over a reflector is that, generally, it is a more powerful source of light. However, this can also prove to be a major disadvantage if you intend to use the available natural light as your primary light source. If the fill-flash is too powerful, greater than the primary source, it will overwhelm the subject and spoil your image.

This problem is less of an issue with modern electronic flash, which tends to feature TTL-metering specifically for fill-in flash situations. However, whether you are using an automatic system or a manual one, it is useful to know the metering technique you should employ.

First, take a meter reading of the area lit by the natural light and note the exposure setting. Then, take a flash meter reading of the area lit by the fill-in flash. Since the aim is for the natural light to dominate, this second reading should be no more than the first. If it is, then you need to reduce the flash output until it is either the same as, or less than, your initial reading. Setting the level of fill-in flash to the same level as the natural light will produce a flat image, so it is better to set the light level from the flash at about one-stop less than the level of natural light. This will help to keep some shadow detail and give your subject dimensional form.

When using fill-in flash, it is better to keep the flash unit off-camera and at an angle to your subject. When photographing people, this will help stop red-eye—caused by the light from the flash reflecting back directly from the retina of the eye.

TIPS

SPECIAL TECHNIQUES

One of the effects you often see created in the daylight studio is a model posed in the striking rays of direct sunlight streaming through a window. Usually, the picture is composed so that some of the surrounding area is included in the shot to create a sense of place. While this effect is a little clichéd now, it is still a highly effective use of natural light in the studio and well worth attempting at some point.

The key is to pose your model so that he/she is directly in the line of the sun's rays. Expose for the rays themselves (best done with a spot meter) and the surrounding area will come out underexposed (darker), giving the impression that the subject is caught in the light, much like a spotlight on a theater stage.

It is not a simple image to capture and may take some experimenting. It is worth bracketing your exposures to ensure at least one of them is exposed as you intended.

7.12 Fill-in flash is invaluable for lightening the subject's dark shadow areas.

7.13 With fill-in flash, keep the angle of the flash to one side to avoid red-eye.

7.13

ARTIFICIAL LIGHT

Ever since the invention of photography, photographers have sought ways to prolong their image-making after the sun has gone down. In the early days, this invention was driven more out of necessity than creative drive. As cameras became more sophisticated and film more advanced, flash took on a whole new life and photographers began creating highly imaginative images with careful and clever use of controlled, artificial light.

Today, the options are boundless. We can have light wherever we go, and lots of it. But, in many ways, learning to photograph with artificial light is far more complex than understanding the nuances of natural light, because there is at least one extra component to consider. It's a little like photographing captive animals, in that people believe it is easier simply because you can control the environment.

What is often overlooked is the difficulty of making an artificial environment look natural. This is a skill that takes time to master and which provides a whole new avenue of creative possibilities.

UNDERSTANDING PORTABLE FLASH

The first experience many photographers have with artificial light is the portable flash unit. And, this is as far as some ever get, put off perhaps by the harsh and unflattering results portable flash can sometimes produce, or by becoming involved in what appears to be a highly technical, complex field of photography. Such reactions are, however, unfounded. Sure, I have seen some appalling photographs taken with portable flash units, but in every one of them it was not the fault of the flash unit, but the photographer. Yes, flash photography can be complicated at times, but no more so than many other areas of photography, such as exposure-control and hyper-focal distance, for example. To ignore the photographic potential that flash creates is to limit your own picture-taking and creative opportunities. Getting to grips with portable flash techniques often leads on to bigger, brighter things.

Types of portable flash unit

Look through the camera bag of any professional photographer, in any field of photography, and you will find some kind of flash unit. And, chances are, you won't find two the same. There are lots of different flash units out there, and you must ask yourself, which is the best one for me?

One way to answer this question is to think about the flash unit in much the same way that you think about your camera. By now you have learned that no single camera can do everything. You may own different camera bodies for different areas of photography. Well, the same applies to flash units, so it makes sense to look through all the options available in order to make an informed decision.

Built-in camera flash

Many modern cameras, in particular 35mm SLRs, come with a flash unit that's usually built into the prism finder. For more serious photographic applications, these units are very handy for quick bursts of fill-in flash, but they suffer from two major problems. Firstly, they are in a fixed position—and not a very good position at that. Being a direct, front-on light source, they give very flat, hard lighting and, when photographing people or animals, will produce the effect known as red- or green-eye. Secondly, they are not particularly powerful and have a very limited range.

8.1 *A built-in flash unit in a modern SLR camera.*

8.2 *Flash from a built-in unit can cause unsightly results such as "green-eye".*

8.3 *Used well, small flash units can add subtle, attractive lights to the subject's eyes.*

8.1

8.2

8.3

8.4

Hot-shoe flash

The vast majority of modern flash units are designed to complement the camera via the hot-shoe (sometimes referred to as the accessory-shoe), which is usually found on top of the prism finder. The hot-shoe provides the electronic link between the flash and the camera, allowing for accurate discharge at the right moment. In some older cameras, the hot-shoe is just an attachment mechanism (an accessory shoe) without this contact point, and the flash is synchronized with the camera via a PC lead. The advantage of this type of flash unit is the often-additional power and range it provides over the built-in version. However, when attached directly to the camera, it suffers the same directional shortcomings as the built-in unit, producing only hard, front-on lighting.

Some of the more advanced units enable bounce-flash, which goes some way to overcoming this problem, although not without some compromise. It is also possible to attach these units off-camera with a specially designed bracket. Synchronization with the camera is then achieved via a PC lead, although some manufacturers make brackets that have the same functions as the on-camera hot-shoe.

8.4 *A portable on-camera flash.*

8.5 *Hammerhead flash.*

8.5

Hammerhead flash

From the name alone you begin to get a feel for this type of flash unit. The hammerhead flash is designed to work off-camera and consists of a large flash head mounted on a stem that acts as a handle. The most compelling feature of this type of flash unit, as its name suggests, is power and range. However, they also boast fast recycling times and a wider choice of accessories, which greatly increase the possibilities for practical application.

Hammerhead flash units are far less portable than the more compact hot-shoe mounted alternatives. But their additional benefits make them the preferred choice of many professional photographers, particularly working in the fields of press, PR, forensics, and wedding photography.

8.6

Ring flash

Ring flash is a specialized type of flash that produces very distinctive all-round, near shadowless lighting. It is commonly used in close-up and macrophotography and attaches to the camera via the front of the lens, which then pokes through a hole in the middle of the flash unit. Synchronization is via a PC cord and adaptor that fits into the hot-shoe. Larger versions are available and are often used by fashion photographers.

8.7

8.6 *A ring-flash unit, often used in macrophotography.*

8.7 *A hot-shoe on the prism finder of an SLR camera, to mount portable flash units.*

8.8

Slave flash

Slave flash units are so called because they work off a main flash unit—most likely your main camera flash. Small and very limited in power, they are generally used to provide fill-flash to the main flash unit, or to create specific lighting effects. They work through a built-in sensor that detects the flash of the main unit and then sets off the flash of the slave. They are very useful accessories and can help to overcome some of the limitations of portable flash units, particularly helping to fill in dark shadow areas caused by the point source of the principal unit. However, they have no direct influence over exposure control so you must calculate exposure manually.

Tilting and rotating heads

Many of the modern portable flash units feature a tilting and rotating head, which, when attached to the hot-shoe, enables positioning of the head and therefore the direction of the flash light away from the main subject.

Now, you may be wondering why one might want to do that. The answer is related to the size of the light source and the quality of light. As I've already indicated by describing types of flash unit, one of the main drawbacks of portable flash units is that, when used in their normal set-up, they produce very hard, flat lighting. Of course, if that's the effect you're trying to create then that's OK. However, if, for instance, you are trying to photograph a subtle portrait then it's a problem.

8.8 *A tilt-and-swivel flash head in the swivel position.*

8.9 *A tilt-and-swivel flash head in the tilt position.*

8.9

One solution is to bounce the flash off a reflector of some kind by rotating the head sideways or tilting it upward. This reflector may be a purpose-made reflector or it could simply be the light-colored wall or ceiling of a room. What you achieve by doing this is to increase the size of the light source from a point source (the straight flash) to an omni-directional source. As with natural light, this will reduce contrast and soften the light, giving a much more natural and appealing affect, particularly for portraiture. For more on bounced flash, see page 165.

And, yes, there is a compromise. By moving the head from its normal position you may lose any TTL-flash metering capability the unit features, which, while problematic, is not insurmountable.

8.10

8.11

8.10 *A slave flash sensor, used to trigger flash when not attached to the camera.*

8.11 *Tilt the flash toward a light-colored wall to reflect light on to the subject to reduce contrast and produce a softer effect.*

Diffusers

Another way to increase the relative size of the light source from a portable flash unit is to attach a diffuser. This may be in the form of a simple, translucent plastic cover that fits directly over the flash head. You can also get larger, more sophisticated versions that resemble scaled-down versions of studio soft boxes, or simply make one yourself using a suitable framework and some white material, such as nylon.

With a diffuser, there is no need to angle the flash and it remains pointed directly at the subject. The diffused light will be of a softer quality than the non-diffused flash, although probably less soft than bounced flash. Another advantage of this is that diffusers can be used with fixed-head flash units. Calculating exposure may or may not be a problem, depending on the flash unit being used.

Direct–attached reflector cards

An alternative to reflecting flashlight off a wall or ceiling is to bounce it off a reflector card. Reflector cards attach directly to the flash head and can be bought commercially or made with relative ease. They consist of a piece of card (usually white but they can also be silver or gold), which varies in shape and size; the larger the card the softer the quality of light reflecting from it. The card is attached to the back of the flash head with sticky tape or Velcro, and the flash head is tilted up so that it fires onto the reflector card.

The advantage of using a reflector card over bouncing flash off a wall or ceiling is that the distance the light travels between the flash head and the reflective surface is usually less and so flash power is maintained. The level of diffusion, however, will generally be less since the reflective surface of the card is much smaller in area than that of a wall or ceiling.

CHOOSING A FLASH UNIT

When choosing a flash unit you must first consider what you are going to be using it for. For example, the typical portable flash set-up for macrophotography is quite different to the one you would use for reportage. Flash units are much like cameras—no one size fits all and when deciding what is best suited to your style of photography you need to consider some of the fundamental features of all flash units. These include power and coverage, recycling times, and levels of automation and dedication to your camera body.

Power

The power of the flashgun is one of the first things you are likely to consider and, as a general rule, the more powerful the flash unit, the more flexibility you have when using it. Power is measured by the flash unit's

guide number, which varies depending on the ISO rating (equivalency) of the film or photo sensor being used. In a nutshell, the bigger the guide number, the more powerful the flash and the greater its range. This increases your flexibility in exposure settings. For example, let's say that you are trying to photograph an athlete running in a stadium. Because you can only get so close, you are unable to influence exposure settings by moving closer to the subject. So, with a less-powerful flash unit, you will probably be shooting at a wide-open aperture and relatively slow shutter speeds, which are not the ideal settings for fast-action photography. However, increase the power (guide number) of the flash unit and you are able to use faster shutter speeds without needing to get closer to the action. The other element of power to consider is that you can always reduce the power of the flash unit down from its maximum, but you cannot increase its power above its maximum. It's better to have more than you need than not enough.

What power buys you then is flexibility. The downsides tend to come in two forms: price and portability. Power costs money and, typically, the higher the guide number, the more expensive the unit. Power also means extra size and weight, and more powerful units tend to be bigger and heavier in size than their smaller cousins. So, once again it becomes a question of balance and compromise. As a rule, go for the biggest gun you can afford.

NOTE

I mentioned that the guide number (GN) of a flash unit varies, depending on the ISO rating of the film (equivalency of the sensor) used. Be aware of this when manufacturers and salespeople quote you guide numbers. For example, a flash unit with a GN of 120 for ISO 400 film is less powerful than a flash unit with a GN of 40 for ISO 25 film. This is a common technique used in sales to make less powerful flash units appear more powerful than they actually are.

8.12

8.12 & 8.13 *When choosing your ideal flash unit, first consider what you will be using it for. If your flash photography is restricted to use indoors for spontaneous portraits such as these, rather than for professional usage, you may simply require a built-in or small, dedicated flash unit. As long as your flash can create enough light for your subjects, creates pleasing effects, and be used to freeze action, this may be all that you require.*

8.13

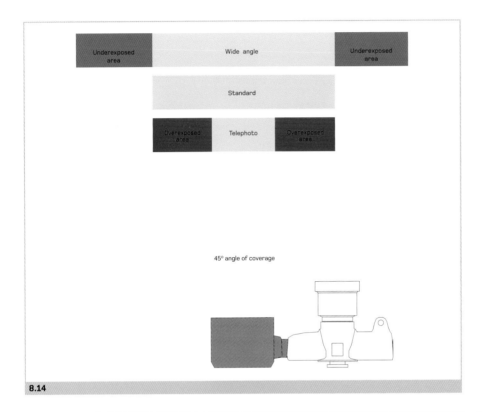

Underexposed area | Wide angle | Underexposed area

Standard

Overexposed area | Telephoto | Overexposed area

45° angle of coverage

8.14

8.15

8.14 *If you use a wide-angle or a telephoto lens, rather than a standard 50mm lens, the coverage of light emitted by your flash will vary, as shown.*

8.15 *A built-in flash unit will offer you adequate light for most everyday photography, but for more wide-ranging photography, a dedicated flash will prove more useful.*

Coverage

When designing photographic equipment, manufacturers have to draw a line in the sand and, with flash, that line dictates that the coverage of the flash (how far it spreads out from the point source), is roughly equivalent to the field of view of the human eye (or a 50mm lens in 35mm photography). If, however, you are using a wide-angle lens with a greater field of view, or a telephoto lens with a narrower field of view, then anomalies will occur. For example, with wide-angle lenses, the flash won't reach all parts of the scene and some vignetting (darkening of the corners of the frame) will occur. With a telephoto lens, some of the light from the flash will be lost, which can throw out your exposures or light areas of the scene that were not part of your composition.

There are a couple of ways to overcome these issues. Some flash units come with a built-in diffuser that widens the angle of coverage of the flash. A better solution, however, is to buy a flash unit with a zoom head. The zoom, which works by way of a fresnel lens in front of the light tube, can be set so that its angle of coverage matches the lens in use. There are limitations, though, and the coverage usually ranges between 28mm—105mm focal lengths. In some more sophisticated (and expensive) models, the zoom function is automatic and changes when you swap lenses or focal lengths. Other systems may operate on a manual basis.

Recycling time

The recycling time of a flash unit measures how quickly the flash tube recharges after it has been fully discharged. You may recall the days when flash units fully discharged with every shot, and then had to wait several seconds for the little red indicator light to come back on, telling you that it was ready to take another flash picture. Things have changed since then, and most flash units only discharge the exact amount of light needed to give a technically correct exposure for the scene, allowing for more continuous shooting. However, recycling time is still an important factor in some specialized fields of photography, particularly when you want to take several shots in quick succession, such as with wildlife, motor sports, and press photography.

Automation

Something that often used to put people off flash was the need to calculate exposures manually based on a table or set of tables that came with your flash unit. Not only was this complicated but very unproductive. Modern flash units have taken much of that complication out of flash exposure and have made life far simpler for the photographer.

An automatic flash unit relies on you telling it the film speed (ISO equivalency) you're shooting at and, in return, it tells you the aperture to use, given your distance from the subject, which it learns from your focus setting. More sophisticated models even give you a range of apertures, together with the range of the flash with each, giving you a little added flexibility.

This system works fine so long as you stick to the indicated settings. If you change anything without consulting the flash unit, however, the flash will carry on regardless and you will end up with technically inaccurate exposures.

DEDICATED FLASH

And so we come to the most evolved of modern day flash units—the dedicated flash. Dedicated flash units communicate directly with your camera and take the information they need to calculate the relevant settings directly, without any need for input from you. With all this information to hand, the flash unit will set shutter speed and adjust output levels depending on your preferred aperture.

In order to work, dedicated flash units need to be used with cameras that have been designed to work with them. So, for example, a Nikon dedicated flash unit will not work on a Canon camera, and vice versa.

BASIC TECHNIQUES

On-camera or off-camera?

With very few exceptions, I would always advise using portable flash off-camera. With lighting coming from directly in front of the subject, particularly hard flash lighting, your images will tend to be flat and lifeless. When photographing people with on-camera flash you will also need to deal with red-eye. Many animals, too, also suffer from something I refer to as "demonic eye"—a phenomenon similar to red-eye but where the eyes turn a shade of bright green. Using the flash unit off-camera, both on a bracket or even hand-held, gives you far more flexibility and will produce much better lighting. Because the light is coming from the side, it will help to give your subject a three-dimensional appeal and form. If you have no option but to use the flash on-camera, then I would advise using it in combination with a diffuser or a reflector card to help soften the quality of the light.

8.17

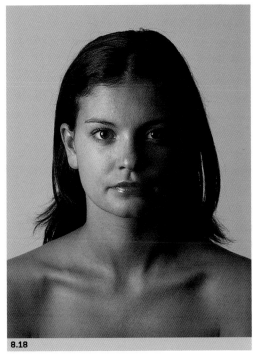

8.18

8.17 *Direct, front-on lighting does not flatter the subject in portrait photography, creating flat images and dark, hard shadows.*

8.18 *Side lighting helps give form to three-dimensional subjects, improving the composition, but in this case, the hard quality of the light makes for a very contrast-rich image.*

Red

Bou
I ha
adv
tec
a n
the
In
to
an
a b
to

Br
be
pe
th
th
re

Ce
th
lig
i.e

8.19

8.19 & 8.20 *Using on-camera flash with a reflector (8.19) or a diffuser (8.20), however, will help to soften the quality of light and give a more pleasing effect than direct light from a point source.*

8.20

Re
Re
fla
dir
the
fur
Th
hig
th
th
wh
ex
to
th
bu
th

A
o
a
s
c
s
r

8.30

8.31

8.32

8.33

The role of the shutter
The first thing you need to do is leave behind some preconceptions about general photographic exposure. Principally, shutter speed plays no influential role in flash exposure. That is not to say it is irrelevant or unimportant. The shutter speed will influence areas of the scene not lit by the flash, since those areas are relying on natural light and will be governed by exposure in the normal way. However, the main relevance of shutter speed in flash exposure is related directly to the flash synchronization speed.

Flash synchronization is specific to cameras with a focal-plane shutter. Some cameras (mainly medium- and large-format), operate leaf shutters, where the shutter is built into the lens and flash synchronization is possible at all shutter speeds. The focal-plane shutter is built into the camera and consists of two shutter curtains—one to begin exposure and one to end it—that travel horizontally or vertically over the film aperture. At very high shutter speeds, the second curtain will begin to close the

exposure before the first curtain has traveled fully across the frame, which is how shutter speeds of thousandths of a second are achieved. Effectively, this creates a slit of light through which exposure is attained. This is where the problem begins. In flash exposure, the duration of the flash effectively acts as the shutter speed. To the naked eye, flash duration can seem a relatively long time. In reality, however, flash exposure usually lasts no more than 1/1000th of a second, and can be even quicker. At these speeds, if the shutter speed set on the camera is too fast—in other words, beyond the pre-set flash synchronization speed, then the only part of the film/photo sensor that will record light is that visible through the tiny slit between the two shutter curtains as they respectively open and close.

So, when using a camera with a focal-plane shutter, which includes most modern cameras, you must set the shutter speed of the camera at the maximum synchronization speed available (usually 1/60th, 1/125th or 1/250th of a second, or slower).

The role of the lens aperture
Lens aperture, then, plays a very influential part in flash exposure and, together with flash duration and distance to subject, is one of the controlling factors. Working with lens aperture, it is possible to control exposure in one of two ways: either by keeping a fixed lens aperture and altering the power output of the flash unit to suit, or by altering the lens aperture and keeping the power output fixed. Whichever option you choose will be governed by flash-to-subject distance and depth of field.

Flash-to-subject distance
Because of the inverse square law, flash-to-subject distance is a key ingredient in the calculation of exposure. The further away from the subject the flash is, the less illumination the subject will receive, and the less flexibility you will have with setting lens aperture (because shutter speed is, to all practical purposes, fixed). So, if you want to work with smaller apertures then you will need to move the flash closer to the subject. But why not just keep the aperture open at its maximum setting and work with that? The answer, of course, lies in available depth of field.

Depth of field
Lens aperture controls the amount of depth of field you have to work with. The wider the aperture, the less depth of field, and subjects in front of and behind your point of focus will not be sharp. This may not be a bad thing. For example, with portraits you may want the background to appear out of focus so it doesn't detract from the main subject. But what happens if you're shooting a scene where front-to-back sharpness is important? Then you will need to close down the lens aperture to give greater depth of field.

8.30 & 8.31 *Flash-to-subject distance is a key ingredient in the calculation of exposure. The further away the subject, the less light it will receive, and vice versa.*

8.32 & 8.33 *The amount of control you have over depth of field is dictated by the power of your flash (8.32). A more powerful flash increases your options for the lens aperture you use, thereby increasing your flexibility on how much depth-of-field you require (8.33).*

The role of the flash unit

Automatic flash units work by measuring the amount of light falling on the subject and cutting off the flash once the exposure has reached its optimum level. How much flash is needed will depend on flash-to-subject distance and the set lens aperture. Sounds simple enough, but it has a flaw. Just like all light meters, the sensor in the flash unit is calibrated to give a technically accurate exposure for a mid-toned subject. If the subject is lighter than, or darker than mid-tone, then your flash-calculated exposure will either underexpose or overexpose the image. So, just as with non-flash exposure, you will need to make adjustments for non-mid-toned subjects. With an automatic flash, this is done by opening or closing the lens aperture from the suggested setting—opening it for lighter-than-mid-toned subjects and closing it for darker-than-mid-toned subjects. With dedicated flash units you can simply dial in the relevant level of exposure compensation on the flash unit (plus for lighter-than-mid-toned subjects and minus for darker-than-mid-toned subjects).

Manual flash exposure

If you are working with a non-automated flash unit or if automatic flash exposure is inappropriate for artistic or technical reasons, then you will need to calculate flash exposure manually.

The first point to remember is that flash exposure is calculated based on the flash-to-subject distance. This differs from natural light exposure calculations, which are based on camera-to-subject distance. Of course, with flash units set on the camera's hot-shoe, camera-to-subject and flash-to-subject distances will be the same. Knowing the range of your flash unit is important because if the flash is too far away from the subject then your pictures will come out underexposed. The first step in calculating flash exposures, then, is determining the range of your flash unit.

You will need to know the guide number (GN) of your flash unit. The GN is given by the manufacturer and refers to the amount of light generated by the flash unit at a given ISO.

With the manufacturer's GN and the base ISO rating, you can then calculate the GN for different film speeds. This is best done working in stops using the f/stop series of numbers. For instance, let's say your flash has a GN of 80 for ISO 100 film. To calculate the GN for, say, Fuji Velvia 50 film, first calculate the difference in stops in film speed. Fuji Velvia 50 is one stop slower than ISO 100 film. For the purpose of calculation, drop the zero from the original GN (80), giving you 8, and apply this to the f/stop scale: f/8. Now, open up one stop from f/8 (because of the slower film speed) and you have f/5.6. Multiply by the zero dropped earlier in the calculation and you get a guide number of 56.

Next, refer to the table, opposite, to work out all the calculations you need for working out manual flash exposure.

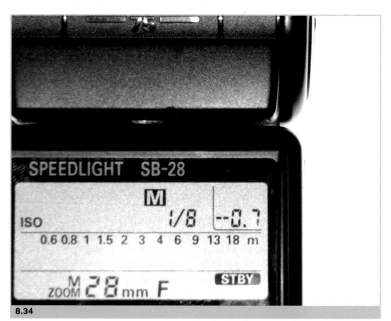

8.34

8.34 *The sensor in your flash unit is calibrated to give a technically accurate exposure for a mid-toned subject. You will need to work the exposure out manually if your subject is paler or darker than a mid-tone.*

Now you know the GN of the film (or ISO equivalency) you are using you can calculate flash-to-subject distance using the following formula:	Flash-shooting distance	=	guide number (GN) ÷ f/stop (lens aperture)
Working with my example above, take your GN of 56. Let's say that your set lens aperture is f/16. Your flash-shooting distance will be 3.5m (around 11ft).	56 (GN) ÷ 16 (f/stop)	=	3.5m (11ft) (flash shooting distance)
Now that you have this base calculation, you can determine where to position the flash based on your preferred exposure settings. For instance, let's take the above example a step further. Say you want to shoot at f/8 rather than f/16. Where do you position the flash unit? Using the above equation, the answer is easily calculated.	56 (GN) ÷ 8 (f/stop)	=	7m (23ft) (flash shooting distance)
Of course, there will be occasions when you are unable to move the flash unit closer to the subject, so you must alter the lens aperture instead. This can be done using a slight variation of the above formula.	Lens aperture	=	guide number (GN) ÷ flash-to-subject distance
Keeping with the above example, let's say you can only move back a distance of 5m. The calculation would be, as follows:	56 (GN) ÷ 5 (meters)	=	f ÷ 5 (m)

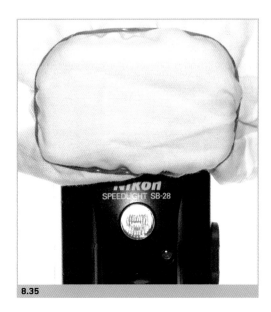

8.35 *A do-it-yourself diffuser for your flash.*

8.35

TESTING FOR ABSORPTION

1 Set your camera with flash attached on a tripod and compose your subject.

2 Take a picture using the manual exposure-calculation method. This will give you your base exposure.

3 Now attach your diffuser and take several more images, opening up the aperture by a half stop each time. Make a note of the aperture settings for each frame number.

4 Once the images are processed, review them to see which one is correctly exposed. Refer to your notes to find the lens aperture setting for that image and then deduct the difference in stops from your base setting. This will tell you the absorption value of the diffuser material in f/stops. For example, if your base exposure was f/11 at 5m and your accurately exposed test shot was f/5.6, then the diffuser material is absorbing two stops of light (f/11 to f/8 to f/5.6 minus two stops).

Now, every time you use that diffuser you will know to open up your manually calculated exposure by two stops.

Calculating flash exposure with bounced flash

How to calculate exposure when bouncing the flash off walls or ceilings will depend on the type of flash unit used. Automatic TTL-flash will do the necessary calculation for you as it measures the light entering through the lens, (subject to any compensation required for non-mid-toned subjects). Similarly, non-TTL auto flash should give a reasonably accurate exposure so long as the light sensor on the flash unit is pointing at the subject.

If you are calculating flash exposure manually, then the same rules apply as those stated on the previous pages, except you must now calculate the exposure based on the total distance the flash has traveled, i.e. the distance between the flash head and the reflective surface, plus the distance between the reflective surface and the subject. In addition, however, you will need to add some compensation for the light lost through absorption and scatter.

Here's another example. Following the example on the previous page, you are now five meters from your subject but decide to bounce the flash off a wall that is three meters from you and four meters from the subject. The total flash-to-subject distance is around seven meters so your calculation would be 56 (GN) ÷ 7 (meters) = f/8. Allowing for light loss and scatter, I would apply a compensation factor of plus one stop giving a final lens aperture of f/5.6.

Calculating flash exposure with bounced flash | Calculating flash exposure with diffusers
Calculating exposure for fill-in flash

175

Calculating flash exposure with diffusers

When using a diffuser, the flash-to-subject distance remains the same but light is lost as it passes through the material of the diffuser. Once again, with TTL-auto and auto-flash units, so long as you do not obscure the sensor, the flash unit will take into account the level of lost light.

With manual calculations, you will need to run some tests to ascertain the exact amount of light being absorbed by the material.

Calculating exposure for fill-in flash

Calculating a sympathetic exposure for fill-in flash requires achieving a harmonious balance between daylight and flashlight. Even with modern auto-TTL flash units I would advise against relying on the system fully to get it right.

The problem with auto-fill flash is that the camera will give as near a balanced result as possible. That is, it will emit enough flash to render the shadows the same brightness as the highlights. This is all very well, but it will create flat lighting with little or no definition or form. A better effect would be an image where the shadows were half as bright as the highlights, creating some contrast and substance in the photograph.

This means that you have to limit the level of flash emitted from the flash unit. With auto-TTL systems this is achieved quite easily by setting exposure compensation to minus one stop. You can go further and darken the shadow area to a quarter of the brightness of the highlight area by setting exposure compensation to minus two stops.

With auto-flash, the technique is slightly more complicated, but is simple enough once you've learned the basics. Firstly, select a lens aperture. Next, take a light reading of the highlight area of the subject and set a shutter speed that will give a correct exposure. If the shutter speed is faster than your flash synchronization speed, you will need to reduce the shutter speed and close down the lens aperture by an equal amount. Once again, this will give you an exposure balanced equally between natural light and flash light.

To reduce the flash output by half, close the aperture down by one stop and reduce the shutter speed by one stop. This will achieve the desired result without affecting the exposure for the natural light.

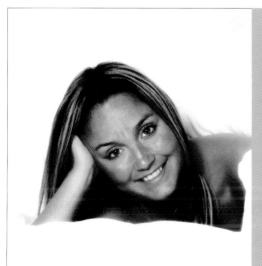

PHOTOGRAPHING WITH ARTIFICIAL LIGHT

1 It is the attachments fitted to the flash head that provide the creativity in studio photography.

2 When photographing using artificial light, remember the inverse square law applies.

3 A lighting ratio of 3:1 gives an excellent balance between highlights and shadow areas and gives your model a three-dimensional form.

4 When photographing people or animals, it is usually best to light from above the eye line.

5 Generally, lighting coming from an angle is preferable to lighting coming from directly in front.

6 Use panel reflectors to provide fill-in light to shadow areas.

7 Light from a diffused source is soft, while light from a point source is hard.

ADVANCED TECHNIQUES

Slow-sync flash

Most of the time, flash pictures are taken with the camera set to its fastest synchronization speed (1/125th of a second). While this allows you to capture the main subject in well-lit conditions, the background is usually underexposed and lacking in detail. Sometimes, you want to achieve this effect, particularly if the background is drab. However, you will mostly want the background or surrounding areas to be well exposed.

The route to achieving this is slow-sync flash. As its name implies, with slow-sync flash the shutter speed is set to a much slower setting to enable the ambient light to record on film. An example would be children having a snowball fight late on a winter's day. Taken under normal flash conditions of say 1/125th second, the children would appear well lit but the background would be dark and featureless. By setting the shutter to around 1/8th second, the action of the children throwing snowballs would still be frozen by the flash, but the background would receive an exposure four stops longer, giving enough time for the film to record detail.

Rear-curtain sync

Flash units are programmed to fire at the beginning of an exposure sequence, that is, when the front of the two shutter curtains open. There is no particular reason for this other than a historical one relating to the technical practicalities of flash bulbs. The downside of this system becomes obvious during long exposures of moving subjects taken with flash. Let's use tennis as an example. A picture of a tennis player serving a ball, taken with flash set at front-curtain sync, would immediately freeze the motion of the racket. Any blur caused by ambient light after the flash had fired would then appear in front of the frozen image of the racket. Naturally, this does not sit well with us. We expect to see the blur appearing behind the racket, depicting forward motion. After all, that is what we consider normal. By setting the camera to rear-curtain sync, the flash will fire at the end of the exposure sequence, giving us an image that we perceive to be the right way round.

8.36

8.37

8.36 & 8.37 Where normal flash can produce dark backgrounds, slow-sync flash, reduces the shutter speed, thereby increasing the amount of light, and revealing better background detail in the picture (8.37).

8.38 & 8.39 If you shoot a subject using flash synchronized to fire when the shutter curtain opens, it can appear back to front (8.38). By using rear-curtain sync, the flash fires at the end of the exposure, which makes everything appear normal again (8.39).

8.38

8.39

STUDIO LIGHTING

Many of the principles of portable flash photography can be carried over into the studio. But the studio also opens up a whole new gamut of opportunity. It is a photographer's playground, where every essence of a photograph can be constructed from scratch. Studio lights are to photographers what brushes are to a painter.

It is important to set the scene. Studio lighting should be considered as two separate components that resemble the relationship between the camera body and the lens. The camera body is simply a dark chamber that holds a light-sensitive material. It is the lens that controls perspective and artistry. With studio lighting, this same relationship is shared between the flash unit and the accessories that complement it. Many people get caught up in the speeds and feeds of technical parlance surrounding studio heads. But, in reality, all they do is emit light. What controls that light and manipulates it to create the desired effect has little to do with the flash. In studio photography, perspective and artistry are controlled by the attachments.

Thus, while not ignoring the technicalities of the lights themselves, this chapter concentrates more on how to get the lights to create the results you want.

9.1 *Self-contained studio monobloc.*

9.2 *Generator pack floor unit that operates several independent flash heads.*

9.3 *Continuous light source (in this case a fluorescent unit designed to work with digital cameras).*

LIGHTING SET-UPS

When setting up a studio, or when deciding what equipment to hire for a studio shoot, there are many things to consider. For instance, what type of lighting are you going to use?

Flash heads

While studio flash heads fulfil the same basic role as portable flash, they differ in many ways. Studio flash units tend to be much larger and, since they run off mains electricity, are far more powerful. They recharge more quickly and, importantly, they can be used with an amazing array of accessories that allow you to radically alter lighting effects. Another very useful feature is that they also come with a modeling light that allows you to see how they will light the subject before they are discharged, giving you far more creative control over your composition. Two main units are available. Self-contained units (monoblocs) that incorporate all the electronics in the flash head, and the generator pack configuration that operates from a separate floor-standing unit to which the flash heads are attached. The latter are generally intended for heavy duty, professional use.

Continuous light sources

We tend to think purely of flash units when discussing studio lighting, but continuous light sources, such as tungsten and fluorescent lighting, can play an equally important role. It would be easy to categorize continuous light sources as the poor man's relation to flash units, but to do so would be wrong. What is important to understand is that flash lighting and continuous source lighting have developed from very different backgrounds, and so direct comparison can often be unfair. You'll find a table of the pros and cons on the page, overleaf, to help guide you.

9.4

9.5

9.4 *Studio monoblocs come in many sizes, depending on your power needs.*

9.5 *With a self-contained monobloc, the electronics are built into the individual flash head.*

Tungsten lamps

You are probably most familiar with tungsten lighting because almost every household is lit by tungsten bulbs. If you have ever taken a photograph using daylight-balanced film under tungsten lighting, you will have noticed that the result is very orange—almost as if it had been shot outdoors during a particularly colorful sunset. This is because tungsten lighting has a color temperature very close to that of sunlight at sunset. Typically, there are two types of tungsten lighting: low-cost hot lights and professional tungsten lighting.

9.6

9.6 *Universal spotlight.*

Low-cost hot lights

So called because, quite simply, they *are* very hot, hot lights come in various strengths, including the 500W Photo pearl (about ten times more powerful than a 100W household light bulb), to the lower wattage but more powerful 275W and 500W Photofloods, which are equivalent to around 8 and 16 domestic 100W light bulbs respectively.

Typically, they are used in conjunction with a reflector, the design of which can vary the quality of light from hard to soft. They can also be used with a diffuser, though you need to be careful when doing so. The heat generated by these lights can be quite intense and it is not unheard of for poorly selected or ill-placed diffusers to go up in flames.

Heat also causes another problem, particularly when photographing people or animals. While these lights may appear to be quite bright to the naked eye, they are less so to light-sensitive photographic material and so need to be used relatively close to the subject you're photographing. If left on for any length of time, your model will look rather hot, and may need a break. Similarly, certain still-life subjects may literally melt before your eyes.

Professional tungsten lighting

Professional tungsten lighting hails from the movie world and, until recently, individual lights tended to be designed for very specific purposes. While these types of tungsten light are still available today, you are far more likely to hire them than buy them and, considering their weight, size, and cost, you would probably only do so for a very special reason.

As manufacturers have become more aware of the commercial opportunities within the photographic market new, photo-specific designs have been released. This new generation of professional tungsten lighting is much smaller than its forebears and uses lamps in the 600W—1,000W range. Typically, however, these pro' lights tend still to be single-function lights (spot, flood, or "trough"), and are less versatile than other options.

Fluorescent lighting

Another form of continuous light is the fluorescent light, which works on the same principle as the fluorescent strip-lighting you see in many homes and offices. Like tungsten lighting, fluorescent lighting gives an intense color cast if used with daylight-balanced film, except that, whereas tungsten has an orange color cast, fluorescent lighting sheds an unpleasant green. While this can be overcome with color-correction filters, it is useful to note that different films react differently to the same fluorescent source, and so you may need to do some testing to obtain accurately balanced results.

The main attraction of fluorescent lighting is its softness, which can complement portraiture work. However, it can turn into a disadvantage if you need a hard light source. Unlike tungsten lighting, fluorescent lighting runs cool and suffers from no major heat problems.

CHOOSING THE RIGHT LIGHTING EQUIPMENT

With such a wide choice of lighting options, you may be uncertain which route to take when choosing what's best for your style of photography. Many people will make their decision based on the power of a particular system, thinking, "System A is 100W higher than System B, so I'll take System A." While this isn't wrong, it excludes an important factor in the decision-making process.

There is a tendency with photography for people to get caught up in the technology of the systems rather than to focus on what is the most important element. The question should really be, "What am I actually trying to achieve?". The problem with basing decisions purely on technology, without any reference to your end goal, is that you are allowing the equipment to dictate how you operate. A better decision would be to visualize in your mind the sort of pictures you want to make, and then choose the best equipment for the job.

Pros and cons	Advantages	Disadvantages
Studio flash	Versatile, with a wide range of lighting-effect accessories.	Can be more expensive than some forms of continuous light source.
	Cool-running. Can be left on for long periods of time without overheating.	Can seem complicated to use for the novice.
	Balanced to natural daylight.	Modeling light gives an idea of the lighting effect but actual flash exposure can vary the effects.
	High-powered, giving more exposure options and greater depth-of-field.	
Low-cost hot lights	Relatively low entry cost.	Low-powered and need to be relatively close to the subject.
	Simple to use, making them ideal for studio beginners.	Hot-running, inclined to overheat quickly.
	What you see is what you get (WYSIWYG).	Need to be balanced with color-correction filters if used with daylight-balanced film.
Professional tungsten lights	Ideal for specialist applications.	Often need to work at maximum apertures and shallow depth of field.
	What you see is what you get (WYSIWYG).	Single-function makes them inflexible.
		Expensive compared to low-cost hot lights and some flash set-ups.
Fluorescent lighting	Ease of use makes them an ideal tool for learning the ropes.	Need to be balanced with color-correction filters if used with daylight-balanced film.
	Cool-running, which means they can be left on for longer without overheating.	Cannot be mixed with flash lighting.
	Newer models have largely overcome the shortcomings of older versions.	Practically, can only be used as a soft light source.
		Flickering can cause poor effects in the final image.

Power

Power will be one of your major considerations. However, power costs money and a good choice could save you hundreds of dollars. When you buy power what you are really buying is flexibility. The more powerful the system the more options you will have setting lens aperture for exposure and the greater will be your control over depth of field. Bear in mind, too, that power is relative to the size of your studio. A light that would be lost in a studio the size of a warehouse may be more than adequate in a studio based at your home. There is no need to waste money on power you'll never need to use.

Ease of use

Another important part of your equation is how easy you find the equipment to use. It's all very well acquiring an all-singing, all-dancing system, but unless you can get it to do what you want, you'll never achieve the results you're after. This is particularly important if you are relatively new to working in a studio. Getting to grips with new techniques can be frustrating, and that can easily turn to disillusionment if you spend more time reading technical manuals than actually taking pictures. Not only that, if you're working with a model, he or she will quickly lose patience and that will show in your photographs.

Versatility

No doubt your subject matter and the effects you are trying to create will change from one day to the next. Therefore, any system you acquire should be able to match your varying needs, both in the immediate and the longer term, as your photography develops and the demands you make on your equipment increases. When examining a studio lighting system, give some thought to how you can expand it in the future and whether it is capable of delivering different qualities of light. Again, this is important if you are just starting out in studio photography; the needs of the novice are likely to alter more radically than those of an experienced pro who has already gone through the learning process. It is also an important financial point, as choosing the right system at the outset—one that will grow with your photography—will negate the need for expensive trade-ins later down the line.

Reliability

The reliability of the system you're working with is a key consideration. What I mean by this is not simply whether the system works when you plug it in and switch it on, but how frequently the lighting element in the unit will need to be changed. There is nothing worse than spending hours getting your shoot set up, and paying for a model, only to find that your bulbs keep blowing.

Back-up system

In my mind, the available back-up system (the accessories you employ in order to alter the lighting effects) is by far the most important element in any decision you make on choice of system. After all, a light is really just a light. How that light falls on the subject, however, and how it can be manipulated for artistic exploitation and creative advantage is entirely dependent on what you are able to put in front of the light.

CHOOSING ACCESSORIES

Studio lighting needs to be managed. It needs to be told where to go and how to fall, much like directing actors in a play. How adept you become at directing your light will go a long way in determining the success of your pictures. At your disposal are an array of accessories that will help you. Quality of light, size of source, contrast, spread, and direction are all within your direct influence.

Reflectors

Studio lighting reflectors, which are also referred to as dish reflectors (because they are shaped like dishes), attach to the front of the flash head and produce a hard, directional light. They come in a variety of sizes and shapes, each having a particular role to play.

Wide-angle/umbrella

The wide-angle/umbrella reflector, also known as a "spill-kill" reflector, creates a very broad, even light source. They are designed for use with umbrellas, where the design complements and enhances the performance of the umbrella. They can also be used to fill broad areas with light. Usually small in size (around 15cm/6in), they create harsh shadows and high-contrast lighting.

Power | Ease of use | Versatility | Reliability | Back-up system | Choosing accessories
Reflectors | Wide-angle/umbrella | General purpose | Key-light

185

9.7

9.8

9.9

9.10

General-purpose

General-purpose reflectors have an even coverage and high light output. Depending on the size (usually around 21cm/8in), they produce medium- to high-contrast lighting.

Key-light

Key-light reflectors are designed to allow high f/stops. They have highly polished surfaces that can be one or two stops brighter than general-purpose reflectors. However, this brightness comes with a downside — the polished surface produces high specularity and contrast.

9.7 *Barn doors.*

9.8 *Wide-angle or umbrella reflector.*

9.9 *General-purpose reflector.*

9.10 *Key-light reflector.*

9.11

9.11 *When using two or more flash units, reflectors can be combined to produce the desired lighting effects. Here, high-performance and key reflectors were used together.*

9.12 *High-performance reflector.*

9.13 *Grid reflector.*

9.14 *Grid diffuser.*

9.15 *A grid diffuser was used here to produce a combination of soft and hard light that adds to the appeal of the picture.*

9.12

9.13

9.14

High-performance

High-performance reflectors are about power. They are designed to concentrate large quantities of light and to maximize light output. They are particularly good at bouncing light off ceilings and lighting large groups of people. Lighting quality tends to be softer than that produced by smaller reflectors.

Grid

Grid reflectors create a number of interesting lighting effects by creating very controlled pools of light, each giving a narrow coverage but without losing intensity. Again, depending on size, they can produce high-contrast lighting, but fall-off is relatively smooth.

9.15

9.16

9.17

9.18

Soft-light

The large size of soft-light reflectors (typically around 40cm/16in) produces a very broad, even light source, soft in quality (as you might expect), which is ideal for fashion and glamor work, used close to the subject. However, removing the inner diffuser can increase brightness.

Sunlight

Sunlight reflectors are designed to replicate sunlight and are ideal for photographing subjects such as architectural models. They produce a broad beam of light and retain relatively high output levels. Without an internal diffuser (built into the soft light, described above), the light will be brighter and higher in contrast.

9.19

9.19 *Adding soft light accessories to the flash unit helps to create a soft quality of light that reduces contrast and softens shadows.*

9.16—9.18
Soft-light reflector (9.16), Sunlight reflector (9.17), Super soft-light reflector (9.18).

9.20 & 9.21
Ring flash (9.20), and back-light (9.21).

9.20

9.21

Ring light

Ring light is often more closely associated with close-up and macro photography, but large, powerful units can be equally employed for studio portraits. The effect is similar to having a large light source directly behind the camera. However, ring light is considerably more symmetrical. It is placed in front of the camera, with the lens poking through a centrally positioned hole in the flash unit.

The lighting effect from ring flash is highly distinctive, and when exposing for a subject lit with ring flash, you may want to overexpose by one or two f/stops so that the resulting image doesn't appear flat.

Back–light

Back-light reflectors produce a natural oval vignette of light, ideally suited to illuminating backgrounds for portraiture.

9.22 *Ring lighting is often used by studio portrait photographers to produce an appropriate style of lighting for this genre.*

9.22

9.23

9.24

9.25

9.26

Snoots

Commonly used in a secondary role to complement the main light, snoots produce a narrow beam of light that can be used to highlight key features of your subject. For example, they can highlight a model's hair, or pick out a brand name on a product or product packaging. The downside to snoots is that, while they produce a very defined, hard-edged pool of light, they also create a secondary ring of softer light around the primary light. They also reduce the brightness of the light quite considerably, sometimes by up to two stops. However, this can be turned to your advantage if you're working with flash units that have a limited power output range. With low-range output it is sometimes impossible to reduce the level of light low enough to create very subtle highlights. Adding a snoot may solve the problem because of this large loss in light.

Honeycombs

A Honeycomb is a metal, lattice-like grid that fits onto the front of the flash head and blocks all illumination on an axis other than straight forward. Honeycombs can be acquired with different cell sizes, and the smaller and deeper the cell, the greater the degree of blockage. The real advantage of a honeycomb is to minimize illumination falling in areas you don't want it to, and they are perhaps even better suited to highlighting very specific areas of a subject than snoots.

Barn doors

Most lighting accessories are designed to limit light spill in areas you don't want illuminated. The simplest accessories for achieving this are barn doors. Barn doors are made up of two, or more usually four, metal flaps hinged to a framework that fits over the light unit. By moving each flap, you can concentrate the light into the areas you want illuminated and block light from those areas you want to be in shadow. When using all four flaps together, you can "funnel" the light into specific areas, much as you would with a snoot.

Fresnel lenses

Fresnel lenses create that classic Hollywood style of lighting. They can achieve very tight control of the direction and size of the light beam, and are ideal for commercial product photography, as well as classic portraiture. Fresnel lenses are also one of the most efficient concentrators of light and can be used to gain high f/stops when needed.

9.23 *Snoot.*

9.24 *Honeycombs, for use with grid reflectors.*

9.25 *Barn doors.*

9.26 *Fresnel.*

9.27 *Spotlights are directional, and emit a narrow beam of light that can be used to highlight specific parts of a scene or subject.*

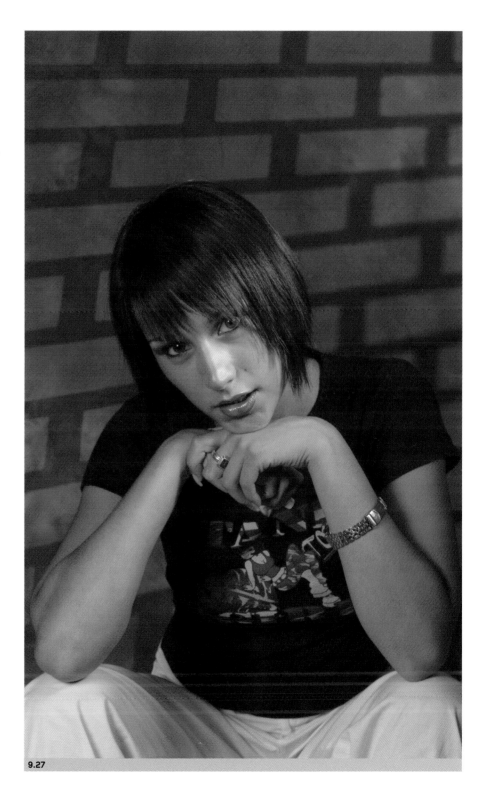

9.27

Umbrellas

Umbrellas, or "brollies", are arguably the photographer's most well-used accessory, and one of the first items you should acquire after the flash head itself. Like reflectors, they come in various sizes and with different surfaces. In addition, different colors are available, including white, silver, and gold.

An umbrella acts as either a reflector or a diffuser, depending on which way the flash head is pointing. With most types of umbrella, the flash head is turned away from the subject, and light is bounced back onto it (in other words, "reflecting" the light). Other umbrellas are made from translucent material, and are designed for the flash to fire through them, to act as diffusers.

The surface color will affect the quality of the light falling on your subject. White, the most popular color, produces soft, non-directional lighting. Metallic—silver and gold—umbrellas, produce a much harder, directional light, which increases contrast. Additionally, a gold surface will give a warm color cast to your subject.

The main advantages of umbrellas are their low cost, combined with high versatility, which makes them ideal for anyone starting out in studio photography. It is possible to get dual-sided versions that are white on one side and either silver or gold on the other. And, since they can be folded down, they save space and are highly portable.

9.28

9.28 *Large, multicolored studio umbrella.*

9.29 *Small studio umbrella and square soft box.*

9.30 *Small, square soft box.*

9.31 *Large, square soft box.*

9.32 *Hexagonal soft box.*

9.33 *Large, round soft box.*

9.29

9.30

9.31

Soft boxes

Soft boxes are designed to produce an even spread of soft, diffused light. The effect is similar to that of indirect sunlight entering through a window. Like reflectors and umbrellas, they come in different sizes, from relatively small to very large. Generally speaking, the larger the box, the softer the lighting.

But this will depend on where the soft box is placed in relation to the subject. For example, if you move a small soft box close to the subject then it can produce lighting equal in quality to a larger soft box placed further away.

Better-quality soft boxes are made with an internal translucent diffuser that sits between the light source and the external material to produce even distribution of light across the whole surface, which is critical for the larger sizes.

The quality of light produced by a soft box makes it ideal for fashion, glamor, and portrait photography, as well as still-life work.

9.32

9.33

BASIC PRINCIPLES OF STUDIO PORTRAIT PHOTOGRAPHY

Lighting ratios

The level of highlight and shadow in a scene determines the lighting ratio. Strong highlight and shadow areas represent a high ratio and indicate a high level of contrast. A more even spread of tones represents a low ratio and indicates a scene with less contrast. A ratio of 3:1 (i.e. the highlights are three times brighter than the shadows), will always give good lighting. However, depending on the effect you are trying to create, you may want to increase or reduce the ratio.

To measure the lighting ratio, first take a meter reading from the secondary light source, making sure that no light spills onto the meter's cone from the main light. Then measure the light emitting from the key light. Finally, measure the light where the sources combine—usually face-on to the camera. The difference in stops between the illumination from the secondary light, and the key and secondary lights combined is your lighting ratio.

For example, let's say that the f/stop rating from the secondary light is f/5.6, and from the combined light sources the f/stop rating is f/16—a three-stop difference. In this example your lighting ratio would be 3:1.

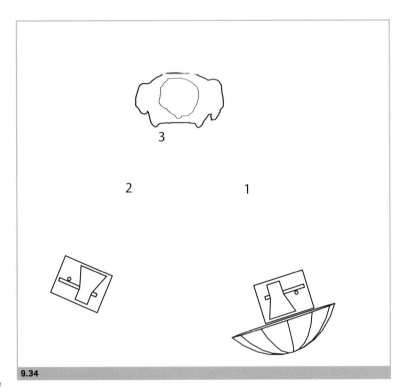

9.34

Spatial relationships

The primary consideration in studio portrait photography regarding spatial relationships is between the subject and the background. The question is whether you want the background to appear sharp and so be included as part of the scene, or whether the background should appear unfocused, and thus be excluded from the main picture.

Whether the background is included or excluded is determined by depth of field, which in turn is determined by your lens aperture, focal length, and camera-to-subject distance. The key to good portrait photography is mastering the art of depth of field in order to provide just the right amount. Too much front-to-back sharpness can reduce the impact of your picture by giving equal weight to objects of secondary importance.

Angle of lighting

We are used to seeing subjects lit, naturally, from above (as though by the sun), even when using artificial light. As soon as the lighting drops below the eye line, the effects can be quite disturbing—especially for your subject!

Lighting-to-subject distance

A common mistake that photographers make is to place the light too far away from the subject. The closer the subject, the softer the lighting becomes, and the greater your flexibility over exposure settings.

Basic principles of studio portrait photography | Lighting ratios | Spatial relationships
Angle of lighting | Lighting-to-subject distance

195

9.34 *To measure the lighting ratio, take readings from the secondary light source, then light emitting from the key light; and, finally, from the point where the sources combine.*

9.35 *Normally, subjects are lit from angles to keep the lighting effects natural, but sometimes you can play with the angle of lighting to create a more dramatic effect.*

9.36 *Try to avoid dropping the angle of light below the eye line, unless you want to achieve this kind of effect.*

9.35

9.36

LIGHTING SET UPS FOR STUDIO PHOTOGRAPHY

Single-light set-up

What can you achieve with a single light? All photographs have a main, or key, light source that provides the energy in your picture. This light gives direction, character, and strength, and all other lights are in dialog with it. Mastering the key light is essential to creating compelling images, and the advantage of starting with a single light set up is that it will help you to focus on this point.

9.37—9.38 *A single-light set up can create very strong, well-defined portraits, and is a good place to start when experimenting with lighting.*

9.38

9.37

9.39—9.42 *With the single-light set up, you can introduce reflectors and diffusers to throw additional light on to the subject.*

9.39

9.40

9.41

9.42

Two-light set up

By adding a second light into the
equation, you can increase your
creative potential and add some
flexibility into the process. The first
light, however, remains the main (key)
light, and this second light will be used
to complement its effects.

9.43

9.44

9.43 & 9.44 *Using a
second light enhances
your potential to shoot
more creative set ups.*

9.45

9.46

9.45—9.48 *A second light in the set up, combined with either a reflector or diffuser can create a softer ambience.*

9.47

9.48

Three-light set up

With the addition of a third light, you can consider more advanced techniques and complex lighting relationships. Notice, however, that the first light that was used is still the main light, and that the two additional lights are working in harmony with it.

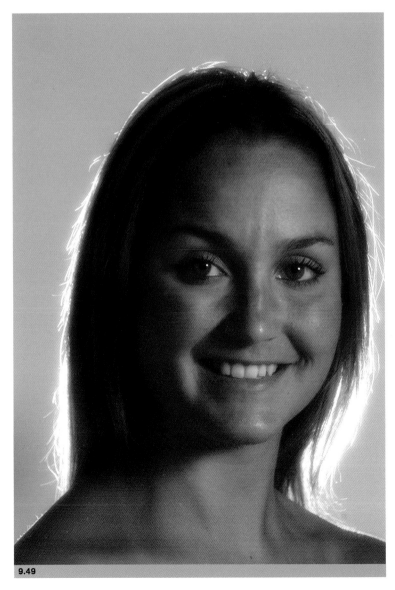

9.49

9.49 & 9.50 *In addition to the main, or key, light, a third diffused light from behind backlights the model's hair for added effect.*

9.50

9.51 & 9.52 *The additional lights, combined with a colored film on the light, sheds a dramatic glow over the subject.*

9.51

9.52

APPENDIX

This short, final chapter contains one of the most essential elements of the book to help you navigate your way around the text—the index—and also the author's and publisher's acknowledgments.

Like many things in life, this book is the culmination of the efforts of team of people without whom this book would not have been possible. In particular I would like to thank the following people for their wisdom, kindness, and generosity over the past few months: the entire team at Rotovision who commissioned me to write the book, and have been with me all the way; Steve Aves and Guy Shirm for their ideas and explanations; Bowens International for the use of their studio, equipment, and images; Jane Nicholson at Intro2020 for her continued support of my work; Ian Webster at Lastolite for the use of images; Paul Harcourt-Davies, whose big knowledge of things little has helped me enormously; and finally to my "home team"—Claire and Josh—who give me the inspiration to carry on.

The publishers would like to thank the following for giving permission to reproduce their photographs in this book: Paul Harcourt-Davies and John Brackenbury for their macro photographs, Tony Blake, Jennifer Dunlop, and Gary, Lauren, and Beth French. Additional thanks are extended to Julia Faiers and Servane Heudiard for their editorial help with this book.